Faith
in
the *Fast*
Lane

Ken Owen

HARVEST HOUSE™ PUBLISHERS

EUGENE, OREGON

Cover by Left Coast Design, Portland, Oregon

Portions of some of the devotions appeared in *National DRAGSTER*, a weekly publication of the National Hot Rod Association. Used by permission.

Photos © 2002 by Gil Rebilas, Mesa, AZ.

FAITH IN THE FAST LANE
Copyright © 2002 by Ken Owen
Published by Harvest House Publishers
Eugene, Oregon 97402

Library of Congress Cataloging-in-Publication Data
ISBN 0-7369-1035-2

Owen, Ken, 1946-
    Faith in the fast lane / Ken Owen.
        p. cm.
    ISBN 0-7369-1035-2 (pbk.)
        1. Christian men—Religious life. I. Title.
    BV4528.2094 2003
    248.8' 8—dc21   2002011962

Printed in the United States of America

03   04   05   06   07   08   09   10   / VP-CF /   10   9   8   7   6   5   4   3   2   1

To my dear friends and colleagues
within the racing community...
to the drivers, team owners and support personnel
who were the inspiration for the thoughts
expressed in this book.

Acknowledgments

Special thanks to Brent Higginson, whose inspiration and diligence made this book possible. I am also very grateful to the wonderful staff of Harvest House Publishers for their kindness and patience in the production of this book.

Contents

ACTIONS

RELATIONSHIPS

part one

ACTIONS

Darrell Russell in Joe Amato's Bilstein-Sponsored Top Fueler

1

Another Fresh Start

If you are like most people I know—especially racers—you probably find comfort in being able to turn the calendar to January every year. It's a new year—a fresh beginning—and an opportunity to put the past behind you and begin looking forward to a new season.

Due no doubt to my background and training as a minister, at the beginning of every new year my mind remembers a little portion of scripture located in 2 Corinthians 5:17 KJV: "...Old things are passed away; behold, all things are become new." I've always been intrigued by that message. What a comforting thought to know that we are given opportunities to start anew. Even though the author of 2 Corinthians was obviously speaking about new beginnings in a spiritual context, it's nice to also have fresh opportunities in other areas of life as well. The past is gone, perished forever. Old things are merely another memory for historians to ponder. One of the keys to understanding this concept is in recognizing that newness must be defined in terms of quality, and not only in terms of time. An emphasis must be placed on the form or quality of any fresh start.

In many ways, new beginnings are progressive transformations. There is a definite point of a new beginning from which springs a progressive development. Oftentimes it is better not to think about what you are, but to focus on *what you are becoming*. Even the natural world around us is a constant illustration of this principle of progressive growth. When we see a magnificent redwood tree, we know that it had a beginning, but we also know it didn't become a fully grown tree overnight. When I admire a brand-new race car, I know the vehicle had a specific point of beginning, but I also appreciate the fact that it didn't become a race car overnight. Parts had to be purchased and pieced together meticulously until that one exciting moment (usually the night before the first race) when that car became a fully developed reality.

As is true in building any race car, no type of process is automatic. You cannot purchase a pile of parts, stash them in your garage each winter, and open the door in the spring expecting a completed vehicle to roll out. Building a race car involves planning, developing, and implementing. There is no easy way around it. Even if you decide to mortgage the house and purchase a complete race car, someone still has to plan it and build it.

This important principle is quite evident in the natural realm, and it is also relevant to the spiritual realm. In a spiritual context we might accurately liken such progressive development to the process of maturity. One of my personal slogans is, "There are no major sponsors in the race of life." You cannot purchase maturity. You have to *build* maturity into your life, and it requires proper resources, sufficient know-how, and the willingness to expend energy and put forth effort. Plus, there is usually a significant cost involved.

I thoroughly believe that goals are important when facing a fresh beginning, and I'm certain that most racers have already established their racing objectives before any new season begins. Perhaps a racer's goal is to qualify for a race for the first time or become a national champion. But remember the obvious—you cannot become a champion after the first race; therefore, your season must become a series of smaller goals, that, hopefully, lead to your ultimate objective. Becoming a champion requires time, planning, and progressive development throughout the course of a season.

Personal maturity takes time, and it will not happen automatically. It must be thoughtfully planned and carefully considered. And don't forget to consider the spiritual side of your life when planning for any new season of your life. After all, without personal growth and maturity, racing (and anything else you care to name) becomes very empty and unfulfilling.

Think about what you want to become. Think about the process of time and the pathway of choices that will help you reach that goal. Then get revved-up and put the pedal to the metal on an exciting life of growth. That always makes you a winner!

Carl Spears' Super Gas Charger at Pomona

2

Rev-Limiters
and Idiot Lights

Let your conscience be your guide. Have you heard that admonition before? Have you ever wondered how effective a guide your conscience is? Well, let's take a look. The word "conscience" is derived by combining the prefix "con" *(with)* with the word "science" *(knowledge)*. Therefore, conscience means "with knowledge." Perhaps a better way to understand the function of the conscience is to define it as an "inborn warning system."

I vividly remember the first time I heard a rev-limiter on a Pro Stock motorcycle. Was I shocked! I was convinced the rider had just blown-up his motor right on the starting line. What a horrible noise. After confidently informing the person next to me of my astute assessment, I was told that it was supposed to sound that way and a rev-limiter would protect the engine from over-revving and ultimately destroying itself. Needless to say, I will never forget the purpose and function of rev-limiters.

Something else I will never forget are the fond memories of the 1960s—those wonderful years when magnificent muscle cars stalked the streets of America and losing my hair was the furthest thing from my mind. Ah, what a great time to be alive! Fast cars ruled, and life was cool. But coolness never comes without a price. As car guys, we, too, had to learn the laws of the land and the ways of the world. As some might express it today, we had to learn the ins and outs of *vehicular correctness.*

I faithfully followed the two fundamental codes of vehicular correctness when it came to purchasing my first muscle car. There were two things a cool person did not want on his personal street machine. Horsepower-robbing air conditioning and idiot lights. Air conditioning was for wimps, and idiot lights were for— well, idiots.

Idiot lights are those irritating little bulbs on the dashboard that so easily ruin an otherwise delightful driving experience by glowing in your face and creating panicked thoughts of mechanical suicide taking place under that sexy cowl induction hood. When that little red light suddenly appeared—the one spelling OIL—my heart would almost stop! In a supremely mocking manner, that light seemed to be saying, "Hey, idiot, you've got a very serious problem here. You better stop and do something!" (Like I actually knew what to do. As you may recall, being cool did not require knowing what to do—only acting like you did.)

The reason they're called idiot lights is that they aren't intelligent enough to tell you what's wrong—only that *something* is wrong. As such, they function like a subtle warning system. In essence, the message is: There's a problem developing, and unless you stop and check out the cause and extent of the problem, you may be in for some serious damage!

Well, that's exactly how our conscience functions in life. God built into us a simple warning system that tries to alert us of any impending emotional or spiritual damage. The conscience isn't specific as to what the source of the problem is; it merely warns that something is amiss, and it may be wise to stop and check things out before more serious damage occurs.

My very first car in life (prior to the aforementioned muscle car of my dreams) didn't have analog gauges, so I was forced to drive a car with—you guessed it—idiot lights. My budget being what it was in those days, that first car was always in disrepair. More often than not, to my embarrassment and disgust, some stupid little red bulb would haunt me day and night. So being the creative little genius that God created me to be, I discovered the perfect solution to those annoying red lights. Racer tape!

Who would have guessed that a carefully placed piece of tape could solve so many problems? Whenever a little red light came on, out came a fresh piece of silver racer tape to cover the light, and—voila!—life was wonderful and trouble-free once again. You see, my adolescent brain easily reasoned that if I could not see the red TEMPERATURE light, my car could not possibly be overheating. Pure and simple. Any guess as to what followed? The next words I remember flowing freely from my mouth at the radiator shop were: "No sir, I really don't remember seeing the temperature light come on."

This particular "idiot" had to learn a valuable but painful lesson. If I chose to ignore the warning light, it didn't change the reality of the situation. By ignoring the light and refusing to stop and evaluate the cause, I became personally accountable for the consequences and the damage incurred from ignoring that warning—and I had the receipts to prove it.

Life is strangely similar. God created you with a conscience, a built-in warning system. Your conscience doesn't explain in detail what problems are developing—only that something is going awry and that any refusal to carefully evaluate the situation could result in serious damage. You can certainly *choose* to override those subtle warnings from within, but the subsequent problems are usually serious. In Acts 24:16, Paul encourages us to strive always to keep our conscience clear before God and man.

Rev-limiters and idiot lights. Both were designed to prevent unnecessary damage. Let's learn to recognize that our conscience was designed to do the same thing. If you ignore its warnings, damage inevitably occurs. If you respond wisely to those warnings, you will save yourself a lot of pain and embarrassment. Take it from one who knows.

Like the idiot light, your conscience may not be able to explain in precise detail the source of the problem, but fortunately there's a reliable solution. Check the manufacturer's manual. From Genesis to Revelation it explains everything.

3

Power Is Nothing Without Control

While waiting for a connecting flight at the Dallas–Fort Worth Airport, I noticed a young man wearing a T-shirt that definitely caught my attention. The shirt was marketing Pirelli Tires and was fully emblazoned with the following statement: Power is nothing without control. While I thoroughly appreciated its creativity as an ad slogan, I was struck by its relevant parallel to what also is a very pragmatic principle of life. As is true with the exciting race cars I enjoy watching week in and week out, *uncontrolled* power is an undesirable experience. The proper application of power is the ultimate objective of *every* driver and crew chief in motorsports.

Producing enough power is seldom the problem. Properly controlling the power is the critical challenge.

Personal maturity demands similar restraints in life. Uncontrolled power, as is often expressed in anger or rage, is not a characteristic highly cherished by many people. Life can be very boring without passion, but passion can be detrimental without proper restraints and moral guidelines. Sadly, self-control and self-discipline are almost lost arts within today's culture, which too often values a lack of behavioral restraints.

Furthermore, it should be noted that there is a very practical difference between self-control and self-discipline. Self-control is keeping yourself from doing what is wrong; self-discipline is making yourself do what is right. Each is essential, and neither one eliminates the need for the other. Yet it's quite easy to confuse the two.

The *American Heritage Dictionary* defines self-control as "the control of one's emotions, desires, or actions by one's own will." The emphasis is on proper *control* through the use of one's determination. In other words, self-control is perfected in our lives by an act of our will. Until we're willing to give self-control a greater manifestation in our lives, it will never happen. Proverbs 25:28 NIV describes it this way, "Like a city whose walls are broken down is a man who lacks self-control."

Self-control means keeping ourselves from doing whatever is wrong, and—according to the dictionary—relates to areas that involve our emotions, our desires, and our actions. But self-control will only be developed as a result of deliberate choice. In case you haven't noticed, self-control does not appear to be humanity's default behavior when no other deliberate action is taken. Moreover, the failure to embrace self-control usually encourages us to put even less restraint on our behavior.

The Pirelli ad people had it right. Proper control is critical to the responsible use of power and strength. The Bible uses another word that is closely associated with the concept of self-control, but it is a word that is very often misunderstood. The word is "meekness," and God's Word characterizes it as "strength under control." Both meekness and self-control are the result of power under proper restraint. Society often equates meekness with weakness, but true meekness requires a significant level of emotional strength and courage. Wimps need not apply.

As many of you may recall, the Bible also promises that the meek shall one day inherit the earth (Matthew 5:5). I have often wondered how this will happen. It's my guess that the meek will merely outlast those who lack self-control.

Referring back to the *American Heritage* definition of self-control, we can also infer that the proper functioning of someone's emotions, desires, and actions is essential to a well-balanced and fulfilling life. Have you noticed how good it feels when you exhibit true self-control? It's a very satisfying and fulfilling experience.

On the other hand, self-discipline is defined as "the training and control of oneself and one's conduct, usually for personal improvement." Now there's a definition that gets me excited. I especially like the part about personal improvement. It's the info that inspires sermons!

If self-discipline involves doing what is right, then we can presume that training and controlling our conduct are essential to the personal improvement we seek. I find it interesting that both training and control are critical elements of self-discipline. Certainly some degree of self-training is necessary before any meaningful control can become evident in one's life.

There are some people in this world who personally resist the idea of greater self-discipline. They believe the absence of control is more in keeping with "moral freedom." To these people, any increase in self-discipline and self-control would be inconsistent with their definition of improvement. Some people clearly cherish the idea of life without moral restraints or behavioral control of any kind. Apparently our friends from *American Heritage* do not agree—and neither does God and neither do I.

Self-control is essential to our sense of self-worth and self-satisfaction. As social beings, we need proper and reasonable guidelines for moral behavior.

There was an interesting study some years ago by researchers who placed a number of children in an open playground. The children manifested a tendency to huddle close together in the center of the playground as they played. However, when the same playground was enclosed by a fence, the children felt more free to play at the outer edges of the area with no apparent apprehension. The researchers concluded that the physical boundaries produced by the fence created a greater sense of security and safety in the minds of the children. Even as adults, we react in a similar way. Most of us prefer some form of moral guidelines and behavioral boundaries in our lives. A lack of boundaries often leads to a greater tendency toward dysfunctional behavior. As a general rule, people want to know what is expected of them. Think about building a race car without a blueprint or any guidelines. Imagine the difficulty in not knowing what rules are pertinent for the race class in which you wish to compete or not knowing the legal limitations with which you must comply.

I am often amazed by the degree of self-discipline I see within racing. Most racers seem to understand the necessity of rules and guidelines, and they are—for the most part—more than willing to work within those boundaries. Let's exhibit the same characteristics when we are away from the track as well.

So take a page from the Pirelli ad book—power is nothing without control, especially when it comes to practicing self-control in your life. And if you begin losing self-control—it's time to get a grip!

4

Be Patient

Be patient. Wait. Easily said—not so easily done. Patience is a virtue desired by all—and we want it immediately if not sooner! But life doesn't always operate according to our time frames or our demands. Patience is a difficult issue in our fast-paced lives. It doesn't relate well to our "pedal to the metal" approach to life. "You snooze, you lose!" Every racer and race fan knows that.

Does having patience mean sitting quietly, waiting for your turn to come up? No way! Consider the farmer. Farming requires a tremendous amount of patience, but have you ever noticed how a farmer waits? Does he sit around doing nothing until it's time for harvest? No. Waiting to a farmer means actively tending to business and constantly maintaining the fields and crops. There is an ongoing preparation for the coming harvest. To a farmer, waiting with patience is by no means passive. Have you ever seen a farmer standing in his field complaining to the land, shouting, "Why aren't you producing yet?" No. The farmer knows he must wait patiently, but he's willing to wait because he knows the crop will come in at the proper time, making the waiting worthwhile.

Furthermore, for which crops does a farmer patiently wait? Whichever crops he planted. If the farmer plants "bad seed," he will receive bad crops. If he plants "no seed," he will get no crops.

But if he plants "good seed," he believes he will receive a good, ripe, full harvest in the fullness of time. In other words, if you want apples, you plant apples. If you want oranges, you plant oranges. Every farmer understands this basic principle, but so often the rest of us fail to grasp it. We plant apples but complain when we don't get oranges. Or we plant no seeds and expect to reap a great harvest. Then we wonder with shock why no harvest is forthcoming. Rather elementary, isn't it? Yet life follows a similar pattern as it relates to attitudes and choices. We indeed reap what we sow.

As with so many issues in life, we must wait patiently for the fullness of time to arrive (the time for harvesting). Have you ever become impatient and tried to eat fruit before it was completely ripe and ready for picking? Do the words sour and bitter come to mind? Once again, the farmer's strength is in his patience.

Perhaps we can learn from the farmer and actively tend to business while waiting for some of life's anticipated results to materialize. For instance, farmers not only need patience for crops to grow, but they also are dependent on events that affect those crops. During biblical times there was an early and late rain that was common to the dry deserts of the Middle East. The early rain came at seed time and the late rain just before harvest time—ensuring a ripe, full crop. Without both rains, the land would not be as fruitful.

It's interesting how most of us view rain as such a negative thing in life. We've all heard the adages that into every life a little rain must fall and it rains on the just and the unjust alike. Perhaps it is true in our lives that life's occasional stormy circumstances come to ripen and mature us more than we know.

What kind of harvest would you like to see in your life? Are you preparing the soil and planting the right seeds? Are you willing to wait out the storms so that the seeds you planted can ripen in the fullness of time?

5

Thingamajigs and Doohickeys

Recently, I began to wonder what might be the world's longest word. Perhaps like many of you, the first word that came to mind was "supercalafragilisticexpialadocious." You remember—that's the word you have to sing in order to pronounce. I never knew what the word meant, only that it related to something quite atrocious. (My apologies to Mary Poppins for not knowing the real meaning.) I was convinced that I knew the world's longest word. Then (in an automotive magazine of all places), I was introduced to this word: Llanfairpwllgwyngyllgogerychwymdrobwlllantysiliogogogoch. For those few of you who might not recognize this word, it's the name of a village in Wales. Yeah, that one. Okay, *now* have I found the world's longest word? Wrong, thesaurus-breath. There's actually a word longer than that one. It seems that a local resident of the afore-mentioned village is known as a Llanfairpwllgwyngyllgogerychwymdrobwlllantysiliogogogochigander, which some of you probably knew already.

If you think your job is tough, how would you like to be a map maker in Wales? Perhaps when the town's youngsters engage in juvenile behavior, they are forced to write the name of their city

100 times on a chalk board. A very long chalkboard. And wouldn't you like to see the uniforms for the local high school soccer team?

Words. What would this world be without them? I suppose there are a few I would like to eliminate from the face of the earth, but all-in-all, words are our amigos, companions, allies, comrades, friends. Some words are unique—not for their size or length—but because no one quite knows what they mean. Two such words are thingamajigs and doohickeys. These words are generic in nature, which is no help at all when you are asked to locate one or the other.

Then there is my mom's favorite word: skoshe. I've learned that it's a measurement of something as in "the soup needs a skoshe more seasoning," but the exact measurement is known to no one at this time. Try asking for a skoshe-size measuring spoon at the store and notice the interesting expression you get from the clerk. Upon further research, I have discovered that a skoshe is somewhere between a dab and a smidgen. For the life of me, I can't imagine a world-class engine tuner ever saying, "We need to add a skoshe more fuel for the next run." Then again, no engine tuner has ever tasted mom's delicious soup, either.

Consider this point of interest. Researchers have estimated that women use far more words each day than men. In fact, on average, a man uses approximately 17,000 words per day, while a woman uses more than 30,000. (This changes, however, on a day when a man wins a race, at which point his word count is subject to a dramatic increase!)

There is certainly a lesson here for men. It seems by some strange quirk of nature that most men utilize the vast majority of their daily allotment of words at the workplace prior to coming home. Unfortunately, the lovely lady in your life still has a significant reserve of words she carries with her well into the evening hours just to share with you.

So no matter how much time has been spent that day on the telephone with her mother, yelling at the kids or chatting with the neighbors, she has lovingly reserved a large cache of words for the moment you walk through the front door. And because your allotment has all but dried up for the day, she is more than willing to offer her extra words in the form of questions designed to extract from you the meaningful dialogue she seeks, while she attempts to exhaust her remaining quota of words. But I'm sure that's a scenario all too familiar to most of you guys.

Consider for a moment the importance of communication in today's world. Now consider the importance of *meaningful* communication. Then consider the consequences of *insufficient* communication. And finally, consider the role that words play in determining the effectiveness and the success of our communications with each other. There are so many important concepts that we need to communicate. For example, love and appreciation need to be communicated openly with those whom we love and appreciate. (Note to men: these would be two of the words your significant other wants to hear during that brief moment of meaningful dialogue when you come home.) How well are you communicating love and appreciation?

Another important idea that needs to be communicated is affection. Society has caused us to be fearful of showing affection to others. People today desperately need affection that is expressed within pure, established relationships—especially families. Are you expressing true affection to those you love?

And all our communication should be based on honesty. The Bible talks about speaking the truth in love, and I agree that honest communication should always be tempered with love and kindness toward others.

Another important principle is commitment. It should be evidenced on a consistent basis, and words (as well as actions) are an integral part of such evidence. Have you ever wondered why governments require an official ceremony before two people are considered married? One reason is that most people will not raise themselves to the level of consistent commitment for promises they never make public. That's usually why a marriage license and some form of marriage vows are required. The purpose of a religious or civil ceremony is for people to *externalize* the commitments they agree to honor. A wedding ceremony doesn't determine the success of a marriage, but it's an important step to begin the process.

And last but not least, we need to communicate thankfulness. Most people I know are very thankful. But most of us (including me) do a poor job of expressing this to others. Yet there are few words that contain as much power as words of thankfulness.

From "thank you" to "I appreciate you," words communicate the deepest feelings and desires of our hearts. Whether long or short, many or few, words are a critical element in communication. So think of words as gifts by which we communicate our soul to others.

U.S. Army Top Fuel Dragster — Tony Schumacher
Miller Lite Dragster — Larry Dixon

6

So What Do You Do?

Have you ever noticed that when people introduce you, they usually do so by describing what you do in life? For example, "I'd like you to meet John; he's a race car driver" or "this is Carol; she works for XYZ Racing." Try to introduce someone without describing what they do. It's more difficult than you might think because once you get past the person's name, it's hard to know what else to say. And unfortunately, after being introduced, you still know very little about John and Carol as individuals.

Since I work a lot with drag-racing people, I know they love to classify things in specific categories. In drag racing, we have a classification for everything and everyone. If you drive a 1958 white Sledmobile coupe with huge fender skirts, we probably have a class just for your car. (Remove the skirts, however, and we'll have to move you up one class higher.)

Needless to say, our society has a tendency to relate to everything in terms of classifications—including people. We forever want to label them and place them in convenient categories. This phenomenon has created an unusual dynamic in that we often grow up trying to find our sense of security in role-orientation. We believe that we need to find the ideal category into which we can place ourselves, thereby becoming (in our thinking anyway) more acceptable to those around us. It's my contention, however, that we would be better off if we related to each other on the basis of who we are instead of what we are or what we do.

The problem for so many of us is that we don't know who we are apart from the roles we portray to others. Perhaps we don't believe people will accept us for who we are. So, we try to hide within the secure images we portray, believing they will please others. Of course, few people ever get to know us for who we really are. Is it any wonder that our society is overcome by superficial relationships?

Have you ever spent much time around professional actors? Actors have a fascinating tendency to relate to each other through the various character roles they have played in their careers, but they seldom interact as the people they really are. I have spent a lot of time with people involved in acting and television, and I have observed this experience on numerous occasions. For the first few years, I found it to be somewhat entertaining, but years later I realized I really didn't know who these people were deep inside, even though I had spent considerable time around many of them. In a strange way, I felt I'd lost something. It made me realize that when we do not (or cannot) relate to one another in a genuine sense, we not only cheat others, but we cheat ourselves as well.

People need to be accepted for *who* they are—not what they are. Unfortunately, our society is not conducive to that kind of acceptance and wholesomeness. Our society's emphasis on personal performance and accomplishment creates severe dysfunctions in the lives of so many people. Furthermore, such an emphasis on role-orientation seldom leads to a healthy understanding of unconditional love. Thus, our most meaningful relationships continue to suffer.

I see this in my line of work as well. Even people of faith can develop a distorted concept of God, relating to him on a performance basis only. A common concern for these people is, "What can God do for me?"

This fascination with role-orientation has many subtle effects upon our relationships and personal encounters. It not only cheapens our friendships, but it hampers our potential chances for meaningful relationships down the road. Even asking someone what he or she does for a living can be misinterpreted as saying, "Tell me why I should be impressed with you." Obviously, this does not encourage people to feel accepted for who they are. There can also be a subtle danger in the way we ask young people what they are going to be when they grow up. Young people may interpret that question as meaning, "What are you going to become someday that will make you important and worth knowing?" In both cases, we unknowingly encourage role-identity.

I must confess that I'm as guilty as anyone in this regard. When I meet someone on an airplane, the first question I inevitably ask is, "What business are you in?" It's as if I'm uncomfortable relating to this person until I have the proper category into which I may place him or her.

Here's a good test to discover if you are susceptible to the temptation of finding your security in role-orientation. If you are enthusiastic about or actively involved in racing, and you are asked to introduce yourself to someone—at what point in your discussion or list of personal descriptions do you include your racing activities? Do you believe racing will increase your credibility or interest in the eyes of those around you?

I always try to help people understand that God wants us to feel special—not just someone lost in a vast sea of humanity. We're uniquely important to him for who we are, not for what we do. Can you imagine God ever being impressed with what we do in life? How would you like to play "one-up" with him? (Picture in your mind God speaking to Sammy Speed-Racer, saying, "When you can go the speed of light, we'll talk.")

Fortunately, we're important to God just the way we are. I believe this is why God says that the very hairs on our heads are numbered. (Out of genuine concern, however, I'm doing my part each year to make it easier for him to count them.) It's God's way of telling us that we are uniquely special to him. It's always encouraging when someone wants to pay individual attention to each need in our lives without regard to our positions or roles. Truly, God's love for us is unconditional!

Our objective, therefore, should be to not identify people based on classification or role-orientation. We shouldn't fall into the temptation of categorizing people and placing them in little boxes. Let's seek to know people for who they are. When you make the effort, you'll discover it's well worth it.

With this in mind, here's an assignment for this week: Try to introduce someone without describing what they do in life. You'll discover a wonderful new level of understanding and appreciation for those closest to you.

Chaplain Ken Owen at NHRA, Las Vegas, October 2002

7

Values...Who Needs 'em?

I am always intrigued by the various perspectives that people and political parties have on the subject of values—family values, social values, economic values, spiritual values and so on. Some people want more values; some want less. What one group embraces as relevant, another rejects as overbearing.

People may say it's not my responsibility to persuade you or convert you to my personal value system (it doesn't mean you can't ask me, though), but I do want to encourage you to at least think about your personal values. For some people, this may begin with the recognition that a value system is necessary. That may seem somewhat elementary, but you would be surprised by how many people cannot tell you what their value systems are. It isn't that they have no values; it's that a consistent and predetermined value hierarchy has never seemed important to them. Of course, if a person can't articulate his or her system of values and beliefs, we can only imagine the behavioral inconsistencies that must be prevalent in that person's life.

What's the big deal, anyway? Why are absolutes important in the first place? Can't a person simply decide to live without being ruled by values and absolutes? Indulge me while I get philosophical for a moment. There are dangers inherent with trying to live your life without a specific value system. For example, when there are no established or absolute values in your life, your behavior will usually determine your values—those values ultimately being a result of what you feel, what you think, and what you do. Therefore, those resultant values will always be unreliable and subject to change because what you feel, think, and do will, by their very nature, be subject to change. This can lead to a frustrating and inconsistent life.

If you do not live by a specific set of standards, your own behavior and the behavior of those around you will ultimately form your future values. And since those values are not developed as a result of systematic forethought and evaluation, the values will in most cases be based on the result of your environment and assorted behavioral influences. Should you prefer to live your life without the restraints of specific values, please be aware that there is a price to pay for this pseudo-freedom. What you feel, think, and do tend to change throughout your life. In fact, with some people these things change from day to day. Imagine the frustration of trying to understand someone like that and keep up with his or her constantly changing values and behavior. Chances are you know people like this—and most likely you are not totally comfortable around them.

Strong relationships thrive when there is a significant degree of consistency and constancy associated with behavior and conduct. We like feeling comfortable around other people, and behavioral consistency allows our comfort level to increase within a relationship. Do you want friends whose values and standards are subject to change at every whim? Do you think people would desire your friendship if you lived your life the same way?

Take the time to consider, evaluate, and clearly define the values and the standards by which you choose to live your life. If you're uncertain about what values are best, I recommend God's

Word. The wisdom in it has worked quite well for more than 2,000 years.

If defining your values is difficult, ask a few of your friends. They will be able to help you. And, as in most cases where value systems are not clearly defined and understood, you may be shocked to discover that your friends see values in your life you might not realize exist. Furthermore, you might not even *want* those particular values evident in your life. Even if you do have a strong value system, you will still find it interesting to ask a friend to define your values as he or she sees them. Again, be prepared for a few surprises. It's always amazing how other people see things in our lives differently than we do.

Values serve an important role in relationships. I am amazed by how often people enter into committed relationships with those who do not share their values. It's as if they do not think that compatible values are important; yet this is one of the most relevant factors in the ongoing success of any relationship.

This is not to say that we cannot have a meaningful relationship with someone unless that person shares every single value that we hold dear. It merely means that we must decide which values are important enough to be given prominence so as to be nonnegotiable in our most serious relationships.

There are other benefits to having clearly defined values. One involves guidance in decision making. Because there is no road map in life, values become our moral compass. For example, there are many decisions in my life that are made according to my moral values. If no clear-cut answer is apparent when various options exist, I usually base my decision on the option that best represents my core values. Without clear values, I would struggle with far more decisions.

Did you know that values often determine the limits of your motivation? Consider this principle: You will never be motivated beyond the limits of your own perceived values in life. In other words, you will always be more motivated by those things you perceive to be of greater value. As you lower values, you lessen motivation. Here's an example. If you don't consider honesty to be an important value, what will keep you from becoming a cheater? (Okay, apart from painful retribution and/or large fines.) Without honesty as a core value, you won't be as motivated to live a life above reproach.

8

Murphy Was a Racer

The following notice appeared in the window of a garment store in Nottingham, England:

> We have been established for over 100 years and have been pleasing and displeasing customers ever since. We have made money and lost money, suffered the effects of coal nationalization, coal rationing, government control, and bad creditors. We have been cussed and discussed, messed with and messed up, lied to, held up, robbed, and swindled. The only reason we remain in business is to see what happens next!

The author of this notice obviously knew life was filled with difficulties, but he was determined to survive, even if only to hope for the best and see what happened next. I have met a lot of people in racing who share the same philosophy as this shopkeeper. Most racers can relate to the fact that they have, at times, pleased and displeased people, made and lost money, been cussed and discussed, and perhaps been swindled on occasion.

Racing can certainly be a cruel taskmaster and a challenging endeavor to mankind's sanity and patience. In a few brief moments a racer can destroy a great amount of money and effort, to say nothing of ego. Races can be lost for the most insignificant of reasons. Weeks of preparation and pampering can quickly be denied by circumstances that must certainly seem unfair to the players involved.

I don't know who writes the rule books for the various racing associations, but I know there is a frequently followed "law" written by some guy named Murphy. His contention is that we should expect the very worst in every situation. Many people believe that Mr. Murphy is seldom wrong in his expectations and prognostications.

The God of this universe also wrote a book of laws, and in it he encourages us to expect the best in every situation, even when that situation appears to be the very worst. I have discovered that if we are not following and living according to God's laws, Murphy's law usually becomes our default philosophy.

No one ever said that life as we know it was fair. And certainly no one ever said that racing was just. But I'm glad that God reveals himself as both fair *and* just. Without a strong trust in God's justness, and without a strong personal belief in him, it's difficult for me to understand how some people survive in today's world of injustice and pain.

This brings us to the big question. You know, the question people want to ask but are afraid they may be struck by lightning for asking. Yep, that one. In case you need reminding, here it is: "If God is such a god of love and goodness, why is there so much pain and suffering in the world? And why does unjustness and unfairness exist in the first place?"

In responding to this question that I have been asked many, many times over the years, I refer to what has become a very special scripture verse to me. In Romans 8:28 we read, "And we know that all that happens to us is working for our good if we love God and are fitting into his plans." This means that no matter how tragic or unfortunate a situation may be, if we will commit it to

God and place our trust in him, he will respond by bringing good from that situation. That's not to say he is responsible for our unfortunate circumstances—merely that he promises to bring good out of them. I don't know how he does it (that's why *he* is God), but I have known it to be true in my life.

What makes God's promise different from Murphy's law is that you are relying on a loving God rather than on circumstances. I would never recommend that anyone rely on life's changing conditions, but I can certainly vote for relying on God for all situations even if they're unfortunate or tragic. In my experience, he offers much better results.

One of the many benefits of serving God involves the rewards that come from his promises. As the God of Romans 8:28, he promises always to bring good out of every bad situation. He promises that we can become better for the bitter if we will consistently submit ourselves to him, commit our circumstances to him, and trust him with the results. I find that to be a much more attractive proposition than what Murphy offers.

Life on this earth is indeed filled with unfairness. This is a consequence of mankind's wrong choices over the centuries. Our hope as Christians, however, is that we maintain our faith through any situation or circumstance and ultimately know God's victory and blessing. In my opinion, one of the joys of remaining in this world is to see what good things are going to happen next!

A friend reminded me recently that "the truths of the universe are universally true." In other words, God's principles of life are consistent and true for all ages. They are trustworthy because he is trustworthy. God is unchanging just as Jesus is the "same yesterday, today, and forever" (Hebrews 13:8). If a person is characterized by negative or undesirable traits, such an inability to change would not be desirable. Fortunately for us, however, the God of the Bible is good, trustworthy, and loving, so we welcome his constancy, his immutability.

There comes a time in the life of every Christian believer when he or she must totally rely on the promise of the truth of God's unchanging character—his immutability—and not succumb to the apparent reality of life's circumstances. The fruit and character of God's personality include love, justice, fairness, mercy, trustworthiness, patience, and much more. As believers in the Christian faith, we rely on him and on the consistency of this universal truth—in spite of what our current circumstances may be. In faith we keep on going; in faith we keep on trusting.

One of the saddest things in life is seeing someone who has lost hope. Hopelessness devastates the human spirit and paralyzes our ability to look to the future with anticipation and excitement. But if your life is founded on a reliable belief system, there is no need to lose hope. There are no hopeless situations as long as we trust in the one who is greater than our greatest problems—our heavenly Father.

9

Walk This Way, Please!

One thing that always makes me laugh is that classic scene by the Marx Brothers. Greeted at the door by an elderly butler, the brothers ask to meet with the owner of the house. The butler, hunchbacked and walking slowly, responds with the following request, "Walk this way, please!" You know the rest—Groucho and clan follow in the steps of the decrepit butler, mimicking his slow, painful walk.

The Marx Brothers, however, are not the only ones trying to mimic someone else's walk. Thousands of young, impressionable racing fans are watching today's racers with intense admiration. Like it or not—racers have become role models for a multitude of star-gazing youngsters who religiously follow our sport with worshipful wonder.

I find it interesting that very few racers I know actually see themselves as role models, and herein dwells a frightening reality. The most dangerous of all role models is the one who is unaware that he or she is being watched in the first place. No doubt during the intensity of battle and the demanding competition we have come to expect within racing, the last thing on a racer's mind is how he or she is being watched by others. But please trust me, it is happening! Even if you're not actively involved in racing, the chances are that someone is looking up to you. When this happens, every move you make, every word you speak (wholesome or otherwise), and every character value you exhibit is monitored and absorbed by young kids who just happen to think you're the greatest thing to come along since they started selling Big Macs at race tracks. Not that this is all bad. Our world in general—and racing in particular—desperately needs positive role models. The issue isn't whether role models exist in racing today, but what kind of role models we are developing. There is a basic developmental need in young people that causes them to seek heroes. This is a God-given dynamic through which young people adequately observe and adopt the important values and qualities necessary for healthy, fulfilling adulthood.

When I look at the kind of role models our current society is providing for this generation, I'm pleased that many of our youth are looking to racing to find their favorite heroes. I'll match racers with anyone in the rock music world or the entertainment industry in quality role modeling. But that's not to say we don't have room to improve. The key element of concern in my opinion is awareness. Racers need to be reminded that they are being thrust into the hero's role whether they like it or not.

I find that very few racers get into racing because they have a desire to become famous or wish to develop heroic reputations. If they did, I suggest professional baseball or basketball as a better venue—to say nothing of the obvious financial benefits. No, racers become racers because they enjoy racing! Whether participating as professionals or amateurs, it appears that very few racers seek the excesses that often come with the territory of risk taking.

In thinking about role models and the influences racers have on their fans, let's look at two categories. Consider the difference between a thermometer and a thermostat. A thermometer *responds* to its environment. It has no direct influence on that environment. A thermostat, on the other hand, controls and determines the conditions and quality of its environment. The interplay racers have with people provides them with similar opportunities. Some people go through life functioning like a thermometer, responding to things around them and ultimately becoming a reflection or mirror image of their surroundings. Other people, however, function like a thermostat—constantly setting the pace and determining the circumstances and the quality of their environment. Guess which one I am challenging you to become?

Remember the old adage, "Do as I say and not as I do?" It didn't work that way with you, and it doesn't work that way with your kids. Our words do not carry the impact that actions and behavior do. People involved in racing and other careers and hobbies proclaim a message by how they live, by what they communicate, and by the values they espouse. Everyone is a preacher of sorts. It's up to us to be the best we can be in modeling Jesus Christ.

Regardless of your profession or interests, I urge you to not settle for being one of life's moral thermometers, being content to reflect the conditions of life around you. Consider the challenge to make a greater effort to positively influence the values of those within your sphere of influence.

To those who are involved in racing, the next time a young fan approaches you to say hello or ask for an autograph, consider what may be going on in his or her mind. Perhaps—just perhaps—the kid is looking to you and hoping your life will say, "Walk this way!"

10

It's About Values, Stupid!

Being a political junkie, I remember well the presidential race of 1992, when one of the more popular sound bites coming from the campaign was: "It's the economy, stupid." In other words, one camp was proudly proclaiming that their platform was built around the issue they considered to be more important to the American people (the economy) than the issue of moral values the opposing camp was trumpeting.

As a result of my many years as a pastor and counselor, I have learned one clear reality: Behavior *always* reflects one's values. Likewise, values are *always* manifested in our conduct and behavior. I have further learned that values give us hope. So strong is this reality that when you take values away from people, you take away their hope. When you remove their hope, you leave them desolate. And before long, you have kids killing kids and other tragic behavior. Disaster is the ultimate result of destroying hope in people's lives. Without hope, our lives become meaningless. Take away my values, and you eventually take away my hope for the future. We cannot survive without some degree of hope in something.

It has wisely been said that there are no hopeless people in life—only people who have lost hope. When people see the insanity and the lack of love in life around them, the natural drive for hope is replaced with anger and frustration. A sense of recklessness and abandon develops, especially in children and teens. Hopelessness leads to selfish behavior—a type of moral self-defense, if you will. That's why a continual lack of values eventually leads to acts of meaningless violence as an expression of extreme frustration.

For the past few decades we have had a liberal element in society that has insisted that moral values not be imposed on others. They say people need to remain free from the restrictive bondage and imposition of such values. And people wonder in shocked dismay when school shootings and senseless crimes take place. I chuckle in sarcastic irony when these same people try to legislate against hate crimes but still refuse to deal with the values and moral issues that lead to that type of behavior in the first place. We will never control hateful behavior until we first control the hate within people. And all too often that hate is the long-term result of a life void of loving guidelines and the moral protection that comes from a strong set of personal values.

How can we insist on not having a formal set of moral values and still be surprised by the predictable consequences? Is this really too hard for people to understand? Or are there too many people who simply do not want to open their eyes to the moral reality of such a critical issue? Perhaps a better way to bring this reality into a more pragmatic perspective is to relate it to our own sport of racing. Would we really enjoy racing if the sanctioning bodies took the view that they didn't want to impose a set of rules and values on people because they prefer racers enjoy the freedom of determining their own rules? I don't think so.

Frankly, I can cope with the challenge of dealing with people who possess opposing values, but what I cannot tolerate is the notion that it is not society's role to teach and impose moral values upon its people. That would be totally inconsistent and absurd. What this world needs is a return to "traditional virtues."

Let me share a few relevant realities that I have learned during my years of life that relate to values. Each of these could be a complete chapter in and of itself, but I'll spare you the commentary. Here are four fundamental realities we should always remember:

- People may doubt what you say, but they will always believe what you do.

- It is unreasonable to expect others to listen to your advice and ignore your example.

- Character is what your actions say when they are in accordance with your stated values.

- To believe means to embrace. To believe a truth is worthless until we fully embrace it.

Years ago I heard a statement that best summarizes one of the major elements of my own personal value system: God above self…people above things. I don't always do a perfect job of living this fully, but it's the goal for which I strive. Politics and national elections aside, life is very precious. It's all about freedoms. It's all about choices. It's all about people. And, ultimately, it's all about values.

part two

RELATIONSHIPS

11

Some Assembly Required

There are many sentences I have come to dread over the years: "Who owns the silver El Camino in the parking lot?" "Do you know how fast you were going, Mr. Owen?" "You shouldn't feel a thing." But the most dreadful combination of words in the English language is: "Some assembly required."

This is not to imply that I'm not handy or adept when it comes to things mechanical. I've built my share of high-performance engines in the past and have initiated enough projects over the years to make "Tim the Tool Man" proud. (Did you notice that "completed" was conspicuous by its absence?) But I really don't consider myself a mechanical wizard. I'm sure that my prowess and aptitude falls somewhere between a greasy shade-tree mechanic and a heart surgeon. However, it occurs to me that there are no shade-tree heart surgeons, so perhaps I fit closer to being a greasy mechanic.

From swing sets to stereo systems, we often find ourselves in situations where some assembly is required before we can totally enjoy the benefits promised to us by a product's manufacturer. And it goes without saying that each of us probably has a unique horror story in that regard.

My most recent project involved the purchase of one of those easy-to-assemble computer desks for the Macintosh computer I use at home. Hey, a few bolts and screws and some glue—who couldn't build one of these? I mean, a 12-year-old could do it! Well, since I couldn't find a 12-year-old to help me, it didn't take long before I was in trouble. Fortunately, with strong perseverance and some muttering, I soon had what most people would recognize as a computer desk. It didn't look like the desk in the catalog, but do-it-yourself projects never do—it's one of those unsolved mysteries of life. Just the same, I was quite proud of my accomplishment, and I always have fun figuring out what to do with the leftover parts. (I wonder if heart surgeons have the same problem?)

You will probably agree that there are many things in life that require some degree of assembly. One of them is relationships—more specifically, the *art of building a successful relationship*. Few things in life promise as much happiness and fulfillment but require as much work and effort to put together properly.

In my role as a minister, I see that broken and damaged relationships are the number one source of pain and stress in today's society. And these same issues affect the members of the racing fraternity because racing is quite demanding at times, thereby creating tremendous strains on relationships. Even in such an intense environment, relationships can be successful and highly fulfilling.

If you ask five crew chiefs how to run 320 miles per hour in a Top Fuel dragster, you may get five different answers. The same is true concerning relationships. There are many approaches to the art of building a successful relationship but, as is true with tuning race cars, two fundamental factors remain constant: some assembly is required (i.e., effort is necessary) and certain principles and absolutes must be followed.

I would like to draw your attention to two absolutes of relationship: purpose and priority. A relationship without significant purpose is doomed to failure. Consider for a moment what forms the basis of a meaningful relationship. Most serious relationships are motivated by common dreams, common values, and common needs. The potential success of a relationship will, to a large degree, be based on the depth and significance of its purpose for being. If the purpose of a relationship is short-term personal gratification, its failure potential will be high. Furthermore, the gratification received from such a relationship typically is short-lived and shallow.

Purpose also leads to greater commitment and inspires endurance. If you eliminate or minimize purpose, you eliminate or minimize the commitment that holds the relationship together. The reality of this concept is clearly evident in our society. When couples announce their engagements, notice how often they plan to remain married as long as they are "in love." Far too many relationships begin with a built-in escape clause, albeit unspoken in many cases. This indication of weak commitment dooms a relationship from day one.

A second key element in the long-term success of a relationship is the priority given to that relationship. This is an area where the racing fraternity is most often vulnerable. To become successful in racing, as in so many sports, demands a high degree of commitment. As long as a couple shares the focus of that purpose and commitment, a common priority exists. However, when one member in a relationship changes his or her priority commitment to the exclusion of the other person, the relationship is clearly on the road to failure.

I'm disturbed by the stress I see in so many marriages within motorsports, especially because racing is not at fault. Many problems come from our occasionally distorted approach to the sport (as can happen in any demanding endeavor) and our failure to continually discuss changing priorities and goals with our partners.

Conversely, when I see relationships within racing (marriage or otherwise) where the goals, values, and purposes are held in common, commitment runs strong. In such cases, participation in racing actually strengthens the relationship. To those people I say, "Amen!"

Perhaps the time has come to consider a tune-up in your relationship. Is it time to reevaluate the purposes and priorities you share with your partner? The results will be well worth the time and effort required. And when you approach the final years of life and reflect on your accomplishments, the fame and fortune you have garnered will seem quite empty in comparison to the comfort and strength that comes from your meaningful and loving relationships. We were created to be relational beings. Don't cheat yourself into thinking that any sport (no matter how rewarding) can ever become a substitute for the loving relationships God intended.

Junior Dragster Raced by Children 8 to 17 Years Old

12

Untrained = Unloved

While recently driving through the streets of my hometown of Gilbert, Arizona, a bumper sticker proclaiming a very intriguing slogan quickly caught my attention. It stated simply: Untrained = Unloved.

Upon closer examination, I noticed that the smaller wording along the bottom of the sticker was advertising a local dog obedience school. Besides the fact that I am a hopeless dog lover, I couldn't help but consider the profound philosophical parallel between the bumper sticker and many aspects of everyday life— on a human level, of course.

Every year it becomes more apparent that we are living in a society that is losing its understanding of unconditional love and the training and discipline such love often demands, especially within the family context.

I remember how shocked I was when I first learned that more than 70 percent of our nation's prison inmates either do not know their fathers or do not have relationships with the men who fathered them. This is cause for concern and reminds me of a profound statement I once heard from a Christian minister who does counseling with prison inmates. He made the statement that he has yet to meet a man in prison who did not hate his father. While

I imagine this is not an absolute reality among all inmates, there is most likely a significant degree of correlation. That 70 percent statistic speaks volumes concerning interpersonal relationships and the consequences of aberrant love.

As a student of the Bible, I've learned the importance of a healthy understanding of the concept of unconditional love. I am amazed as I examine today's society and see how deeply we have lost our perception of this profound truth. With amazing consistency, a lack of unconditional love seems to be at the core of much of the dysfunction and misbehavior in our current society. Moreover, I'm personally convinced that this is one of the critical elements within a family that is most lacking when the parent–child relationship is perverted or severed.

Unfortunately, the reality of unconditional love is not highly regarded or taught today. For the most part, our only understanding of this concept comes from religious teachings and faith-based instruction. This is due to the fact that true unconditional love is a manifestation and expression of divine character and behavior. Thus, the more we remove God and faith-based values from our schools and social curriculum, the less understanding and emphasis will exist on this important topic.

In the shocking statistics mentioned earlier regarding prison inmates and their fathers, it becomes quite sobering to realize that the vast majority of those inmates never had a relationship with a father who was capable of modeling unconditional love—if they even had a father at all during their childhood.

As a brief overview, unconditional love expresses itself without regard to *circumstances* or *behavior*. The key to a balanced understanding of unconditional love is in our response. We must learn to distinguish between a person's behavior and a person's being. In other words, we must realize that we can love someone unconditionally even when we do not approve of that person's conduct or behavior. Too often in our society we see these as being one and the same. Because of this, people are led to believe that if we do not approve of their behavior, we do not approve of them—and, therefore, cannot possibly love them.

Let us suppose that a certain racer is caught in violation of a specific rule and the consequence has to be paid. Let us further assume that the penalty imposed for this particular violation is for the racer to sit out one lap of racing. In view of this judgment, it should not be inferred that the sanctioning body is angry at the racer or no longer approves of him as a person. It merely means that a penalty had to be imposed in order to maintain the integrity of the rules. But it would be incorrect for that driver to assume that he was no longer liked because such action was taken. The same is true in our personal lives and relationships. The imposing of certain consequences does not necessarily mean the disapproval of the person in violation.

Unconditional love teaches that I can love you even while despising your behavior. For a surety, this is taught among many major religions of the world as the means by which a loving God can relate to us in a loving way despite our wrong or rebellious behavior on occasion. And he expects no less from us. Hence, we must be able to transfer the reality of unconditional love to our own interpersonal relationships. This truth is also quite important as it relates to parents and children. Experience has taught us that children who are not raised in an environment of unconditional love will themselves have difficulty expressing that kind of love—unless they experience complete reconditioning and relearning.

As those who designed the Untrained = Unloved bumper sticker will tell you, it is precisely this kind of love that enables us to properly train our pets—even to the point of demanding discipline and giving instruction as a loving choice.

This is the same kind of love that we need to express within human relationships. Unconditional love means that parents will be willing to lovingly train and discipline their children, recognizing that these goals will lead to healthy development and maturity.

I encourage you to actively understand and practice the concept of unconditional love, especially as it relates to your personal relationships. Learn the critical discipline of loving others even when you don't approve of their behaviors. Anything less than that is not true love. Anything less will cheapen your relationships. Anything less will lead to performance-based relationships that will ultimately crumble at the onset of any personal disapproval or dissatisfaction.

Unconditional love accepts a person for what he or she is— not for what the individual does. Therefore, within the context of our most significant relationships, let us learn to discern between a person's being and a person's behavior. Loving relationships may be the most precious gifts God ever gives us in this life. Let's not ruin these wonderful gifts by wrongly reacting to the very people we love the most.

1963 Impala

13

Promises, Promises

A few years ago we relocated our Racers For Christ ministry from southern California to the Phoenix suburb of Gilbert, Arizona. Within weeks of our move, we experienced the beginning of Arizona's fabled monsoon season, complete with fabulous lightning storms and some of the most dramatic cloud formations I have ever seen. We also witnessed something seldom seen in California during the month of July—rainbows.

I have always been a pushover for a beautiful rainbow. As far back into my youth as I can remember, there was a fascination with this particular phenomenon of nature's beauty. And I learned early on that there was special significance to rainbows in the historical account of most religions. You've all heard the story—that God created the rainbow, following a worldwide flood upon the earth during the days of Noah, as a reminder that he would never again destroy the world in a similar manner. According to Jewish history, God established the rainbow as a perpetual token (or sign) so we would be reminded of this covenant promise.

I concluded early in my life that the pot of gold at the end of the rainbow was fantasy, but I soon discovered that the "Plot of God" at the beginning of the rainbow was real. I remember studying how the rainbow represented an unconditional promise to humankind. In other words, faith and trust had no bearing on its fulfillment. It was God's promise to mankind, regardless of our actions or behaviors.

It's amazing what one can remember nearly 40 years after college. I still recall reading that noted scholar and scientist Henry Morris asserted that the hydrological conditions necessary to create a rainbow are conditions that make another worldwide flood impossible. I always considered this tidbit of information quite interesting and comforting. Even as the fossil-bearing rocks of the earth's crust continually remind us that the entire earth was once covered by water, so the rainbow reminds us that this event will never be repeated in earth's future. In the book of Genesis, God is quoted as saying, "I will remember my covenant between me and you....Whenever the rainbow appears in the clouds, I will see it and remember the everlasting covenant between God and all living creatures of every kind on the earth" (Genesis 9:15-16 NIV).

The word "remember" means: "to call to mind to someone's advantage for purposes of good." It also means to celebrate or commemorate, frequently connoting the "affection of the mind" and the action that accompanies such remembrance. When God sees his rainbow, he recalls his promise with affection and, in true celebration, takes appropriate action for our good. In this case, the action for good is to continue honoring his promise to not completely flood the earth again.

We've all made promises to people. How many of the promises you have made over the years still remain unbroken? (I don't see too many hands out there!)

The dictionary defines a promise as a vow or declaration assuring that one will do (or not do) something. We have all been on both ends of broken promises, but promises made—and our ability to keep and honor them—are critical measures of character and integrity.

Promises give birth to hope, and hope is an extremely important element of life. If promises lead to hope, then broken promises lead to a breakdown of hopefulness. I wonder how many parents have heard their children state, "But you promised!" Those three words can form the basis of a breakdown of trust between a child and a parent. And the same is true in any relationship. If promises are broken on a consistent basis, it leads to a complete lack of trust and hope.

I know how frustrating racers get if they believe there is inconsistency in the enforcement of rules and regulations. I have been witness to many occasions when an upset racer approached a race official with rulebook in hand, complaining that a certain rule was being disregarded and was therefore not fair to all the racers. He was reminding the official of something that was stated (promised) in the rulebook; it's his way of saying "but you promised."

The power of a promise is not in the promise, but in its author. Confidence in any promise is based on one's faith in the person making it. Without some degree of relationship (and, therefore, trust) in the promise's author, there is no release of faith and hope in what a promise declares. When we make a promise, we place our reputation on the line for all to see and judge. Our word becomes our reputation.

Most of you are aware of a very prominent men's movement taking place in our country known as Promise Keepers. Promise keeping is not reserved for men only because it's an important foundation to the trust and integrity that must form the basis of any committed relationship.

Even though any major movement will have its critics (and some no doubt justified), I applaud the Promise Keepers program for its concern and commitment to the essential importance of trustworthiness and integrity in the most meaningful relationships of life.

If your word determines your reputation, what kind of reputation do you have among the people who comprise your social sphere? Keep in mind that "remember" means to call to mind to someone's advantage for purposes of good. Do your promises reflect that definition? Do they consider the good of others? Do they benefit those to whom they are made?

May I suggest to you that there is more to be concerned with than our ability to keep promises? I am uneasy about our lack of willingness to make meaningful promises in the first place. I have met many people in life who have decided that the best way to guard against unbroken promises is to simply make none. How unfortunate; how empty.

Don't be afraid to make promises—and don't be afraid to keep those promises. Not only will others benefit by your commitment and integrity, but you will develop a strong and worthy reputation as a person of character and honor. Our world desperately needs more promise keepers.

Every rainbow reminds us that the creator was not afraid to externalize his promise to us. He made sure the entire world knew about it, and he was willing and ready to put his reputation on the line for all to see and judge. I strongly suggest to you that we should do the same. We will never regret it. I promise.

14

Changes in the Whether

There are few things in life that will frustrate a crew chief on a professional racing team more than unexpected changes in the weather. Such changes create significant challenges in the quest for optimum performance.

Likewise, there are few things in life that frustrate us in our personal and professional relationships as much as unexpected "changes in the whether." Never knowing for sure whether a person will do one thing or another definitely creates challenges in the performance of the relationships of our lives. It is unfortunate that we do not have the psychological technology to check a person's "whether report" so that we can have a better understanding of how to approach him or her on a given occasion.

No one enjoys enduring the effects of double-mindedness. Have you been around people who are always changing their minds about things? Have you known the frustration that comes from people who are inconsistent in their beliefs and in their positions on various issues? It's difficult to feel comfortable around people who are capricious or wishy-washy. And evidently God agrees. In the book of Revelation (chapter 3), he chides the ancient church for being "lukewarm" in their actions, indicating that he preferred them to be hot or cold. It's similar to an admonition that was popular during my younger years when people would say: "Do something—even if it's wrong!" In other words, no one wants to deal with indecision. Show some resolve; take some action.

One of the most difficult attitudes for people to tolerate is indifference. In fact, psychologists tell us that the opposite of love is not hate, but a total lack of emotion. You may not like being the recipient of hate, but at least you know what you're dealing with. Not so with indifference. Strangely enough, there are people who can endure a hate-filled relationship, but they cannot remain in a relationship characterized by apathy.

If you were to analyze some of the more successful teams in racing (or any business endeavor or enterprise), you would no doubt find similar key elements and characteristics. Among them would be the ability to remain focused, the ability to have a clear vision, and the ability to follow a plan. What you will not likely find, however, is a spirit of double-mindedness or a sense of indifference to the team's objectives or to the people who are called upon to fulfill those goals.

There are obviously many dangers involved with being in relationships where double-mindedness is present. Instead we should be more like the little boy who was overheard talking to himself as he strutted through the backyard wearing his baseball cap and toting a bat and ball.

> "I'm the greatest hitter in the world," he announced to no one in particular.
>
> Then he tossed the ball into the air, swung at it, and missed.
>
> "Strike one!" he yelled.

Undaunted, he picked up the ball and said again, "I'm the greatest hitter in the world!"

He tossed the ball into the air. When it came down, he swung again and missed.

"Strike two!" he cried.

The boy paused a moment to examine his bat and ball carefully. He spit on his hands and rubbed them together. He straightened his cap and proclaimed with conviction, "I'm the greatest hitter in the world!"

Once again he tossed the ball up in the air, swung at it, and missed.

"Strike three!"

Suddenly he shouted with renewed confidence, "Wow! I'm the greatest pitcher in the world!"

What about you? Are you a person of your word? Are you loyal to the people around you? Are you able to avoid double-mindedness in your life and in your relationships? I encourage you to remain loyal to the crucial causes of your life and to the people who surround you. Remain true to your goals and vision while maintaining a standard of diligence.

Del Worsham Racing His Nitromethane-Powered Funny Car

15

In Search of Commitment

Everyone wants commitment, but very few people seem to achieve it in their personal relationships. And in my years of pastoral counseling, it is evident that strong commitments are more elusive than ever.

As counseling sessions go, my experience with "Joanne" was rather normal. She wanted some advice as she began to prayerfully seek direction for a very important decision in her life. We talked, considered many of the options, and prayed together. She stated with a high degree of confidence that she was committed to the decision she had just made and excited over all that God was going to do in her life.

I saw Joanne a couple of weeks later and asked her how her plans were progressing since our discussion. I was surprised to hear that she was now heading in a totally different direction and was convinced this is what God was leading her to do. What a dramatic change of thought and intention!

I remember well how strongly "Bill" felt about the choice of partners he had just made as he announced his engagement to Susan. It wasn't long, however, before Bill was courting another woman, convinced once again that she was God's perfect choice for his life. Then again, with so much on his mind, it must be easy for God to get confused.

I'm convinced that our world needs to see a *demonstration* of *true commitment*. We've become good at *talking* about it, but we don't always *live* it. In today's world, role modeling shows that true commitment to values and beliefs still exists.

I have learned that without true love as a basis (expressed in unselfishness), there can be no genuine commitment to others. The strength of our commitment to another person will be equal to the level of unselfishness in our own lives. The more selfish we are, the weaker our commitments will be.

Here again is another aspect of the commitment problem common in our society. There's a disturbing increase in the self-ishness of people's behavior within today's world, and this surely will have a negative impact on the relationships that those people attempt to develop during their lifetime.

How do we show our commitment? By externalizing our special commitments—getting them out in the open. We need to make them clearly known, not only to the people to whom we are committed, but to the people around us.

Another crucial element in the expression of personal commitment is our loyalty to the people to whom we are devoted. Commitment means loyalty—loyalty under most circumstances. Often that loyalty is expressed in our forbearance of one another, by our willingness to bear the consequences of wrongs done against us. This is contrary to human nature—and to the world's view of relationship—but it's an essential part of unconditional love.

For many people, loyalty is based on performance; it is based on an "if oriented" perspective. "If you perform as I expect, then I'll remain loyal to you." But true loyalty isn't based on performance. If I am committed to you, and you behave in a way that I do not approve—your behavior will not affect my commitment.

That's why it's critical for parents to express disapproval of a child's behavior without allowing the child to think that their love and commitment have decreased.

Intrinsic to a practical expression of commitment is the belief that people need people. If pride demands that we not develop close friendships—or if our insecurities and past hurts dictate that we isolate ourselves from meaningful relationships—we will never know the joy of true commitment, thereby robbing ourselves of the rich blessings that result from deep, fulfilling relationships.

But let's also examine some of the things that hinder true commitment within relationships.

Fear—a fear of the consequences and responsibilities involved with commitment. When we externalize (or verbalize) an internal commitment, that commitment becomes tangible. And there is a cost to real commitment. There are serious responsibilities involved, which may lead to further fear and tempt us to avoid relationships altogether. We may also fear the abuse and rejection that can result from commitments. The easiest way to avoid rejection is to avoid all commitments. It's not a very healthy solution, but it is certainly effective.

Wrong priorities—letting things become more important than people. Even the idea of commitment can override our actual commitments. We can excitedly talk about commitment, yet never live it.

Affliction and testing—committed people will always run toward a problem and not away from it. Crisis will always prove who the truly committed people are. Have you ever noticed how many people tend to move away during times of affliction and stress? Yet that's when truly committed people are needed the most. Here's a good rule-of-thumb: Never trust guidance received during times of stress, affliction, or testing. Affliction purifies commitments. So remember, commitment never tested under fire may not be genuine. That's why every relationship will ultimately reach at least one critical testing point. At that point, the relationship will either develop into genuine commitment or remain a superficial acquaintance. Superficiality itself also hinders commitment. Society today is filled with friendly people who have no sense of commitment. They have friendliness but not friendship.

Low self-image—the lack of self-esteem is disastrous to commitment. People with low self-esteem are often afraid to make commitments. They question why anyone would want to commit to them, so it's hard for them to commit. Insecurity not only prevents us from ties with others, but it also prevents us from accepting commitments.

Think about three people to whom you are seriously committed. When did you last verbalize your commitment to each of them? Love expressed in commitment must be active—not passive. Energize and activate your commitments in life today.

Strive to implement the following steps of commitment in your life: 1) *define* your commitments (make them clear), 2) *externalize* your commitments (make them known), and 3) *activate* your commitments (make them real).

16

Love Your Neighbor

One of the first moral guidelines I remember learning as a youngster was the biblical injunction to "love your neighbor as you love yourself." Our society has certainly wandered from this principle! Loving your neighbor as yourself is referred to in the Bible as the "royal law" (see James 2:8). This means it's a priestly or divine admonition, further attesting to its high and lofty objective. Therefore, fulfilling this royal law demands that we step above and beyond our normal human level and perspective of relationship (i.e., selfishness) and seek a higher expression of this the greatest of virtues.

Of special significance is the fact that the Bible treats this admonition as a command. We are *commanded* to love others. And herein is a key point: Whenever the Bible commands an action, it is viewing that action as a *choice*—not as an emotion. Today it seems like most people treat love as a feeling, and in this lies the basis for our greatest misunderstanding of this divine concept.

When the Bible commands us to love our neighbor, we are not being asked to develop the warm fuzzies for everyone in the world; rather, we are being asked to make kind and loving choices as they relate to others. Each of us is capable of such loving actions; we only need to be willing to do so. And this includes loving the unlovely. There will always be some people who are more difficult to love than others, but there is nothing that should prohibit us from being able to make love-based choices. It doesn't mean everybody has to become our best friend, nor does it mean we are required to spend time with everyone. It merely means that on whatever level our paths cross with others, we are expected to act in love toward those people. I don't always like it; I don't always do it—but I know I am capable of it. And whenever I fail to express that kind of love-based action, I am clearly violating God's command for my life as it relates to my neighbor. Love is a choice, which is critical to our understanding of love. That's not to say that no emotions are involved, but emotions are not part of the proper definition of love.

Not only is love a choice, but love must be expressed in choices. Consider this profound truth: Apart from choices, love is meaningless. Love *must be* lived out in actions. (Men, ask any woman to explain this.) That's why ladies love to receive flowers on Valentine's Day. It's that special expression and action that proves to her that your love is more than mere words.

Unfortunately, we do not live in a choice-oriented society; we live in a performance-oriented world where love is conditional: "I'll love you as long as you perform according to my expectations."

But the greatest expression of love is *unconditional*—a love that is totally unselfish in nature and motive. Have you ever been in a relationship where you felt you were being used? If so, that was a relationship based on a selfish motive. Unconditional love should form the basis of any successful relationship. There is nothing worse in life than being in a performance-oriented relationship, one in which you feel your only worth is in how well you perform.

I knew a well-known racer some years ago who developed a reputation of being difficult to work for. Such was the plight of

"Jim's" life after being hired to this dream team. In almost every case, the criticism I heard from Jim related to the fact that he and other team members never felt appreciated for the work they performed. There was a low tolerance for mistakes and constant humiliation when something was not done correctly. And, as is often the case in these scenarios, there was never ample praise for a job done well. Before long Jim's working relationship fostered a condition of low self-esteem, and soon there was no further desire to work for his renowned employer. Sadly, Jim never felt any degree of respect or gratitude for his effort. And he never felt any sense of commitment from the person who hired him, which brings us to another characteristic of love—commitment.

We all need to feel we are loved for who we are, not for what we do. The basis of our commitment will always determine the success of the relationship. If the foundation is true love, our commitment will be expressed in consistent, unselfish choices. If the commitment is emotionally based, it will be expressed in constant change, since emotions, by nature, are inconsistent and unreliable.

I'm sure most people agree that there isn't enough *real* love in this world. By that I mean a kind, benevolent caring and concern for others. Therefore, the issue in my opinion is one of stewardship and accountability. Those who have a healthy understanding of love become accountable to others and should feel obligated to do their best to share that love with the world. So if you understand the essence of unconditional love, be a faithful steward of the understanding you possess.

Do others see love being expressed in your life? Nothing in life is as rewarding as the return on your investment of love in other people. Continually choose love as a consistent characteristic of your moral nature. Not only will you be elevated to a higher level of fulfillment in life, but you'll become a tremendous encouragement to those around you.

What does the Bible say about love? First Corinthians 13 is referred to by many as the love chapter. As you read these characteristics, notice that each can only be expressed through loving *choices* that we make.

- Love is very patient
- Love is very kind
- Love is never jealous or envious
- Love is never boastful or proud
- Love is never haughty, selfish, or rude
- Love does not demand its own way
- Love is not irritable or touchy
- Love does not hold grudges
- Love will hardly notice when others do it wrong
- Love is never glad about injustice
- Love rejoices whenever truth wins out
- You will be loyal to one you love whatever the cost
- If you love someone you will
    —believe in that person and expect the best
    —stand your ground in defending one you love

It's my constant prayer that God will give me the ability to express this kind of love to others. Will you accept the challenge and join me in that prayer?

Do you know how to teach unselfish love to others? The same way God did—by demonstrating it. Love can only be taught by modeling, and it can only be accurately evaluated by the actions it prompts. So let's commit to being more effective in our relationships!

17

Doing unto Others

There is a challenging verse of scripture in Romans 12 that most of you have probably heard. The context of this verse is do unto others as you would have them do unto you. The motive behind this passage is found in verse 9, which states, in principle, that love must be sincere. In other words, love is the motivating basis and primary condition for the operation of all spiritual behavior. This particular passage deals with spiritual gifts—and love is presented as the motivating basis in the operation of God-given gifts. A further axiom to this principle is that love always guarantees sincerity. Because selfishness is in fact the opposite of love, selfishness is seldom sincere.

Have you read Romans 12:16-19?

> Work happily together. Don't try to act big. Don't try to get into the good graces of important people, but enjoy the company of ordinary folks. And don't think you know it all! Never pay back evil for evil. Do things in such a way that everyone can see you are honest clear through. Don't quarrel with anyone. Be at peace with everyone, just as much as possible. Dear friends, never avenge yourselves. Leave that to God, for he has said that he will repay those who deserve it. [Don't take the law into your own hands.]

This passage reveals three life-changing principles for human interaction. If you ever become the victim of personal attacks or unfair allegations, I guarantee that these principles will work if you put them into action in your life.

Principle 1: Live in harmony with one another. The word "harmony" means "to be of the same mind as others; to be like-minded." If we don't share a common belief in some things, harmony won't take place. This verse gives us two key elements for living in harmony: don't be proud, and don't be conceited. The literal translation is: "Don't let your wisdom be in yourself." Don't be deceived into thinking that you don't need others—or that your own wisdom is sufficient or all that you need in life. We need each other.

Principle 2: Do not repay anyone evil for evil. The Bible reminds us that our gifts were never intended for evil uses or vengeance but only for doing good to others. Yet how often we are tempted to use our God-given gifts and abilities for harm or vengeance. We must remember that God gives only good and perfect gifts, and therefore only for good purposes or uses. We are further admonished to be careful to do what is right in the eyes of others, not just what we consider to be good and proper. Verse 18 goes on to remind us to "live at peace with everyone." The Bible is telling us that the outcome of all true gifts should be peacefulness. That's our role, because peacefulness depends on us doing our part.

Principle 3: If your enemy is hungry, feed him; if thirsty, give him something to drink. Our job is to care for the needs of others, even our enemies. That's why God gave us gifts in the first place, to focus on the needs of others. Remember, not one of the spiritual gifts described in the Bible is given for us to use on ourselves. True gifts find meaning as we reach out to others.

Verse 21 states what I believe is the overriding principle that forms the foundation for all of our understanding regarding our conduct towards others: *Do not be overcome by evil, but overcome evil with good.* In the context of this chapter, the writer is saying that spiritual gifts are our defense *against* evil and our offense *over* evil. How do we conquer evil? By fighting it with good. The strategy is to respond in an opposite spirit. That's why we're told to love our enemies.

This may be one of the most important principles you will ever learn in life, especially as it relates to relationships and dealing with hurts and personal attacks against your character. The biblical way has never been to fight back in the same spirit. One of the greatest lessons to learn in life is how to fight fairly in the opposite spirit.

Amazingly, responding in the opposite spirit neutralizes your aggressor. When someone comes after you in anger, a soft voice turns away wrath. When someone attacks you with hate, a loving response calms the person more quickly than anything else. Yes, it's tough to do, but with patience and practice, it can be done. And as you do your part (in responding properly to others), God will do his part (the result). Apply this principle to interpersonal relationships, and it works every time! For a better biblical understanding of this particular principle, read Luke 6:27-31:

> Listen, all of you. Love your enemies. Do good to those who hate you. Pray for the happiness of those who curse you; implore God's blessing on those who hurt you. If someone slaps you on one cheek, let him slap the other too! If someone demands your coat, give him your shirt besides. Give what you have to anyone who asks you for it; and when things are taken away from you, don't worry about getting them back. Treat others as you want them to treat you.

The governing principle is quite simple: Do unto others as you would have them do unto you. I believe God operates by the same principle. He will assume that we want to be treated the same way we treat others. It's a function of accountability in life. When it comes to determining how God will treat us, he allows us to make the rules by which he will operate in our lives. Because he is just and fair, he won't treat us in a manner higher than we are willing to treat others.

As it relates to personal relationships and personal interaction, God's desire is that we would live in peace and harmony with others. Racers know well that they will receive their greatest performance when all of the parts of a race car are functioning in harmony and doing exactly what they were designed to do in the way they were designed to do it. When any one part ceases to perform its intended function, the entire race car is affected.

Racers and their crews refer to this ideal level of operation as "finding the right combination." It involves the perfect coordination of functioning parts to maximize the performance capabilities of the race car. When this same principle relates to our personal lives, God calls it harmony. Everybody getting along properly, functioning according to the ways God has gifted them and designed them to perform.

I hope you never find yourself in a difficult situation in which these guidelines become necessary. But if you do, remember these key principles of interaction and relationship. Then pray for those who attack you or seek to bring you harm.

How are you to pray? Ask God to bring about in the person's life the most beneficial result. Then let God determine what that result should be. That's his responsibility; not yours. He will do a much more effective job. I've tried it many times, and it works best when I leave it to him.

part three

ATTITUDES

Rick Hough in His Father's Nanook AAFA

18

No Fear!

When asked if I was afraid because I refused to go skydiving with premier jumper Mark Slater, I responded with an emphatic, *"No!"* I'm not a coward. I just refuse to go skydiving because I understand the gravity of the situation. The way I see it, if God intended for me to fly, he would have given me wings. I do plan to fly eventually, but I prefer to do it as a result of going to *heaven*—not the other way around! And do you know why they call it a "free fall"? Because it's not until you hit the ground that you pay the big price. So I avoid skydiving for very logical reasons. (Okay, that plus the fact that I'm a coward.)

The same goes for bungee jumping. Now there's an intelligent sport. Don't you wonder about the guy who came up with this idea? Talk about being a few feet short of a quarter-mile.

Needless to say, the chances of me jumping out of an airplane or off a bridge are about the same as taking a joyride with my friend and motorcycle stunt rider Krazy Keith Kardell. (The way I look at it is there must be a reason why he's not called Kourageous Keith Kardell.)

Though some of us deny it, we all battle fears of various sorts. In child psychology I was taught that babies are born with only one real fear—the fear of falling. (I told you skydiving wasn't something God endorsed.) Some researchers add the fear of noise as being innate, but all agree on the fear of falling as being with us from birth. That and the fear of not receiving the current issue of *Hot Rod* magazine.

I have two strong fears in my life. The first is the fear of having to go to the bathroom in the middle of a sermon. The second is the fear of not recognizing people at races. I usually walk through the pits at race tracks afraid that I will walk past someone without recognizing who he or she is. I tend to remember people by their names or by their race cars, but not always by their faces. So if I appear to ignore people, I'm not being a snob—I'm just not recognizing them. In this regard, I am currently petitioning racing organizations for a rule that says drivers and crews can never wander more than than ten feet away from their race cars at any time during an event.

Speaking of fears, far too many people have a fear of flying in an airplane (although I think it's more likely a fear of crashing). Fortunately, that one isn't a problem for me. I actually love flying, and I have flesh-colored knuckles to prove it. I'm also amazed by how many racers—upon seeing me board their flight—remark how much safer they feel knowing I'm on the same airplane. If only they knew how much I'm looking forward to going to heaven!

One of the more important principles I've learned regarding fear is that it paralyzes people. Fear is the opposite of faith. Because of this, faith not only neutralizes fear, but it also displaces it in our lives. Throughout life, fears are constantly knocking on the doors to our souls, but as often as we allow faith to open that door, fear will continue to disappear and eventually become nonexistent.

Another principle I've learned is that faith requires an object. We must have faith in something. You can have faith in a parachute, you can have faith in a person, and you can certainly have faith in God. But you cannot just have faith. Therefore, if you struggle with fear, perhaps you should examine what or who is your object of faith. In many cases, people soon discover they are trying to generate faith in and of itself. It doesn't work that way.

A third truth I've discovered is that a strong sense of security minimizes fear. I am often asked during interviews if racers have a fear of death and so attend our chapel services in response to that fear. I find very few professional drivers in whom I sense any fear. Certainly there is respect for their vehicles and respect for the inherent risks in racing—but usually not fear. The drivers feel secure because they're in cars designed with safety and protection in mind.

These reasons are why I am such a strong believer in what the Bible teaches about life and faith. In Proverbs 9:10 NIV we read, "The fear of the LORD is the beginning of wisdom." "Fear" means reverence and respect; therefore, respect for the Lord (and his ways) is the beginning of wisdom. It's the starting line on the journey toward *true* wisdom. If God is the embodiment of all wisdom and understanding (which I believe is true), then he is where I need to begin. The secret, in my opinion, is seeking *him,* not seeking wisdom. God is the object of my faith.

The most effective way to fight fear is to replace it with faith. But as I just noted, for faith to be effective, it must be based on something or someone. If the object of your faith is meaningful, then your faith can be effective in displacing the fears that may be bothering or paralyzing you. If the object is not providing relief, perhaps you need to reexamine your faith and consider a new approach.

Abnormal fears serve no positive purpose in life. They paralyze us physically, spiritually, and emotionally. My desire is for you to find freedom from fears by replacing those fears with courage and faith. Perhaps it's not politically correct in today's society to refer to people as being "afraid," but if you see yourself as being "courageously challenged," please know that help is available. It was Franklin Roosevelt who once said, "We have nothing to fear but fear itself." Then again, Roosevelt never went skydiving.

19

Anger... It's Quite the Rage

Congratulations! You made it past the chapter title. Some people, upon reading this headline, will have tuned out by now. For many people, the subject of anger and rage hits a little too close to home. So thanks for hanging in here with me.

Anger in itself is not necessarily bad. It can be a very necessary and useful reaction. Many psychologists have stated that there are no damaging or destructive emotions per se. All emotions we are capable of experiencing are constructive when used properly. All emotions, however, can become destructive when we fail to express them in harmony with our created limitations. Anger can be appropriate as a communication of feeling in reaction to another person's behavior. But it can also get dangerously out of control.

Racing provides many opportunities for the improper expression of anger and rage because it demands the expenditure of intense concentration and emotional energy. Under the stressfulness of these factors and in the heat of battle, tempers can (and do) get out of hand. Perhaps the most dangerous war zone in racing is being within a helmet's throw of a losing driver.

While it is true that every racer must learn how to deal with defeat and disappointment, not everyone has learned to handle these elements with a proper manifestation of emotion. (That's merely a nice way of saying that too many of us are still losing our cool far too often and need to learn a little more self-control.)

From my earliest years of religious training I can remember hearing about "righteous indignation." But even righteous indignation becomes unrighteous anger in two ways: 1) by the *ventilation* of anger and 2) by the *internalization* of anger.

These two extremes often are known more popularly as *blowing up* and *clamming up*. When someone blows up, emotional energies are aimed and fired at someone else. When a person clams up, bodily tensions are released within. In both cases, the emotional energy of anger is wasted. In both cases it is used destructively. Ventilating takes place when anger is released toward others or toward a situation without proper self-control. Blowing up hurts someone, but it also hurts the person ventilating the anger. Ventilation may result in the loss of friendships and often destroys significant relationships built upon the foundation of good communication.

Internalization takes place when anger is released within and never expressed properly. When we internalize, our emotional energy becomes destructive against ourselves. We soon become irritable, sullen, tense, and miserable. It also hurts our relationship with others. People who internalize are usually not good company because they often "have it in for others" and may allow problems to come between themselves and other people.

There are numerous proverbs concerning uncontrolled anger and rage, such as—

- A fool gives full vent to anger, but a wise person quietly holds it back (Proverbs 29:11 NLT).

- Like a city whose walls are broken down is a man who lacks self-control (Proverbs 25:28 NLT).

- A wise man restrains his anger and overlooks insults. This is to his credit (Proverbs 19:11).

- Do not associate with a man given to anger, or go with a hot-tempered man, or you will learn his ways and find a snare for yourself (Proverbs 22:24-25 NASB).

Internalizing anger toward others leads to bitterness and resentment, so it is better to confront anger directly. A person controls anger best when he or she is solution-oriented rather than problem-oriented. Problem-oriented people are those who like to talk about a problem, feel sorry for themselves, start blaming others, and focus their energies on who is at fault. The energies of anger and rage are wasted and used in a damaging manner when they are focused on the problem or directed solely toward oneself or another. Solution-oriented people, on the other hand, size up the problem, sort out responsibilities, and turn as quickly as possible toward solving the problem. Moreover, anger expressed in uncontrolled outbursts is improper behavior—at all times.

Anger is a powerful emotion and can be a positive force when used properly. If used properly, anger drives people to begin to rectify any wrong situation involving others. In counseling, a person filled with anger is taught to redirect that anger in a positive manner; the anger is refocused toward a solution and away from rage and bitterness.

When people are willing to seek proper solutions, they will find them. But when they are determined to seek vengeance or vindication, they will not see the best solution. We must separate the relationship from the issue, and then we must rectify the relationship before dealing with the problem at hand.

People can learn to live without bitterness, anger, rage, slander and malice. But they also must develop and maintain attitudes of goodwill toward others. Such attitudes can be sustained only by developing patterns of kindness to one another.

The bottom line is clear. Love must replace anger. It may not be easy, but it is certainly possible. The next time you walk within a helmet's throw of a disappointed race-car driver, pray that he or she will turn the anger and frustration into a positive force for personal growth.

Go Karts

20

Please Don't Be Offended

I was speaking with a friend recently who was explaining an unfortunate circumstance that had befallen him. As he explained to me how someone had taken advantage of him, he remarked how much he was offended by that person's behavior.

The following day I began thinking about my friend's words, and I tried to remember when I was last offended by someone's actions. Suddenly, for the first time in my 56 years, I realized that I never think about being offended by people.

Does this mean people have never tried to offend me? No. Does this mean people have never exhibited offensive behavior toward me? Not at all. It merely means that I do not relate to the idea of being offended. Certainly over the years I have known people to hurt me by various expressions of behavior, and I surely am not immune to the pain that such actions cause. But in spite of being hurt, I don't relate to it or respond to it in the manner of being offended.

I am not suggesting we should not stand up to offensive behavior in other people. Quite the contrary. And do not fall into the trap of thinking that not becoming offended somehow gives approval to the misconduct of others. That is not the case. You are merely controlling your response to the actions of others, whatever they may be. There is a fundamental distinction between the offensive action and our decision to become offended. One does not necessitate the other.

Soon after contemplating this issue, I became aware of many people who seem to go through life being offended at one thing or another, by one person or another. And I realized that this is a very dismal and discouraging way to experience life. Do you know people who fit this description as well? Is it you?

Motor racing offers numerous opportunities for people to be offended. Any activity that involves the interaction of people is ripe with potential. And, whether intentional or not, all people at one time or another manifest behavior that is both hurtful and offensive to someone else. When encountering this painful situation, being offended only hurts you and in no way negates or minimizes the reality of the offensive behavior. So what good purpose does being offended serve in your life? Not one.

Perhaps another person's actions upset you. Perhaps someone's words were offensive to you. Every day brings a number of challenging circumstances for us to face. Unfortunately, you will never be able to control offensive behavior in other people, but you can control your own reactions. That's why we are each responsible for our own actions and not for the actions of others.

Ironically, there is an interesting corollary to this truth. In reality, the more we can control our own reactions to a person's behavior, the more it will (in time) tend to soften that person's behavior. It is similar in principle to the proverb that says "a gentle answer turns away wrath" (Proverbs 15:1 NIV). I refer to this principle as reacting in the opposite spirit. Whenever we react to someone's behavior in a similar spirit, it tends to fan the flames and incite more negative behavior. But when we respond in an opposite spirit, a confrontational situation will usually be defused and neutralized.

You need to be in control of your own life and your own reactions. Why give that power to someone else? I am the one who ultimately controls whether you can offend me. If I choose to not become offended (regardless of the hurtful nature of your behavior against me), you cannot offend me. And by the way, that's not a challenge.

Perhaps you need to ask yourself the same question I had to face. When was the last time you felt offended? How did you choose to allow yourself to be offended in that situation? Was the situation improved by being offended?

So choose the path of greater maturity. Do not allow yourself to be offended. Spare yourself the negative emotions that only burden you and make the situation worse. It won't be easy, but you will be a better person for it. You will also feel better about yourself and improve your ability to control your reactions.

21

This Isn't Fair!

Of obvious interest and importance in racing (and life in general) is fairness. Numerous racers would undoubtedly leave racing if they believed racing events were being operated with favoritism and other biases. Fairness serves as the heart and core of any sport. Without it, motor racing becomes nothing more than a farcical endeavor in futility.

Of deeper concern, however, is an increasing awareness that, although we are doing a good job of maintaining fairness within our sport, we seem to be experiencing a loss of fairness in society at large. It seems that individuals have their own standard based on the specific values by which they choose to live their own lives.

Some might argue that there's nothing wrong with allowing people the freedom to determine their own individual standards of behavior. Unfortunately, too much individuality in this regard leads to a collapse of moral uniformity. And when there is no uniformly accepted standard for behavior in general, people consider fairness in relation to their own standards and circumstances only, without proper regard for others. Sadly, this seems to accurately describe today's society far too much of the time.

The more people are allowed to determine their own individual standards of behavior apart from any consideration of its impact upon others, the more fractured society becomes. Individuals soon become concerned solely with their own lives and what they believe benefits them the most, without concern for others with whom they interact in life. In other words, people determine what they think is fair to them, regardless of its impact on anyone else.

If we were to apply this situation to racing, the consequences become more readily apparent. Imagine the challenge of competing in a category of racing in which each racer was free to develop his or her own standard of fairness. Racer "A" might decide that a 350-cubic-inch engine was fair, while racer "B" might decide that 427 cubic inches was more preferable.

And suppose the sanctioning body's tech department decided that it was the prerogative of each racer to determine what was in his or her best interests. In other words, they didn't want to make people upset by imposing a standardized set of rules that stifled a racer's individuality and uniqueness. I think there might be a few complaints from the rank and file of other racers.

This capricious development of standards takes place far too often within today's world. Society's attempt to remain objective and unbiased as it relates to personal conduct and behavior is creating a total lack of standardization, which will slowly lead to social instability, uncertainty, and chaos.

For instance, children need and desire boundaries and behavioral guidelines as they mature. Even as adults, we function more effectively and more comfortably within an understandable set of standards. While we may not always agree on what those standards should be, most people do agree on the necessity of some kind of standard for conduct and behavior.

I must confess, however, that I do not always enjoy practicing what I preach. A while back I took my 1987 El Camino to have it "smogged" in order to renew my annual registration. While the emission standards in Arizona are far more lenient than what I experienced when living in California, my warmed-over 350 small block failed its smog test.

There are few things in this life that challenge my sense of moral integrity and Christianity more than a failed emissions test. So, true to form as a mere mortal, my immediate reaction was, "This isn't fair!" After all, it had passed with an impressive clean bill of health just two years earlier. And besides, that dumb red pickup truck ahead of me at the testing station was spewing oily smoke every time the engine was revved, and somehow it got through. I demand a recount—a second opinion! Perhaps do-overs would be appropriate. And why hasn't anyone in government ever invented the automotive equivalent of golf's mulligan? (Eventually I discovered that my El Camino failed due to an inoperative EGR valve.)

In spite of the inconvenience incurred and the constant reminder of my disgusting humanity, I learned yet again another important lesson of life. And whether I like or approve of the standards involved, some form of standardization is necessary. So I finally accepted the inevitable, got the part replaced, and passed the test on the second try. I chalked it up to another learning experience. (Do they ever end?)

Regardless of the particulars involved, all of us face similar scenarios every week. We need to relax and not panic. Standards are essential for the reasonable and equitable flow of life.

Whether we're talking about life's daily serendipitous scenarios, the art of championship racing, or passing that dreaded annual emissions test, standards are a necessary part of life from which most people benefit. And look at the positive side—if you're ever in Arizona and happen to get passed by a fast, silver El Camino, be comforted in knowing that the clear blue sky in Phoenix is in no way being jeopardized. Yes, sir, life is good!

22

Having a Gratitude Attitude

One of life's great secrets in terms of happiness and well-being involves a clear understanding of the incredible power of thankfulness. There is a very interesting passage of scripture in the New Testament book of Romans that reads: "For since the creation of the world God's invisible qualities—his eternal power and divine nature—have been clearly seen, being understood from what has been made, so that men are without excuse. For although they knew God, they neither glorified him as God nor gave thanks to him..." (Romans 1:20-21 NIV).

According to this biblical passage, God has carefully revealed himself to all of his creation, (which includes you and me). Each person will ultimately be judged by how he or she responds to that knowledge and revelation placed within. The two most fundamental responses God looks for in mankind—and the most basic standards by which all people will be judged—are glorifying God as God (acknowledging God for who he is) and being thankful.

Thankfulness is perhaps the single most powerful and life-changing attitude known to mankind. But it needs to be out in the open—to be seen and experienced by others. That's why it requires some degree of giving on our part.

As it relates to sponsors, crew members, family, and other key people who make racing possible, thankfulness should be expressed to be most effective. The same is true concerning God. If you are a person of faith, you should externalize and express your thankfulness to him as well.

There is no way to truly understand and acknowledge God's reality and character without also being thankful for who he is and for the life he has given to us. In this regard I have yet to meet the person who doesn't have something in life for which to be thankful. Even if you possess far less than most people, you still have reasons to be thankful. The Bible verses we quoted from Romans 1 state with unflinching conviction that "men are without excuse."

This is one reason atheism is so terrible. A true atheist is limited in his ability to be thankful since it requires an object. If you cannot acknowledge a source for your blessings, how can you feel grateful? If an avowed atheist feels thankful for the lovely weather or a beautiful sunset, he has become a hypocrite because he is denying what God is revealing. That must be an unhappy way to live. I've noticed over the years that ungrateful people are not always enjoyable to be with, and they tend to be miserable. But thankful people are usually pleasant to be around.

Thankful people are happy people. Evidently the ancient Greeks fully understood this principle, as the root word for thankfulness is actually their word for "joy," as used throughout the New Testament. This is obviously more than a coincidental relationship. Have you noticed that it's difficult to be thankful without feeling joyful, and that it's difficult to be joyful without wanting to thank someone? Anyone?

Notice this the next time a race winner is interviewed on television and begins to thank his many sponsors. Do you think racers are paid to express thanks to all those sponsors? Okay, so they are. But winners always want to thank someone, even if they don't have a sponsor. It's a natural reaction to the joyfulness of the moment.

Personal relationships certainly emphasize this principle of thankfulness as well. For example, wives are forever complaining to their husbands, "You don't appreciate me!" What every wise husband needs to learn quickly is that his wife doesn't just care how he feels—she also cares about how he *expresses* what he feels. (Men: For reasons of self-preservation, please reread that last sentence. Trust me—you will be tested on this!)

Most people agree that more people criticize them for their mistakes than thank them for their accomplishments. That's a sad commentary on our society's understanding of thankfulness—or lack thereof. We all have a need to feel appreciated, and we want people to be thankful and grateful for what we contribute. The real issue is not whether we are thankful, but how we express our thankfulness to others.

Furthermore, we need to be thankful in *all* circumstances. This raises us to a position above our circumstances. We may not always be in control of the circumstances in our lives, but thankfulness makes us superior to those circumstances because we are in control of our reactions.

I have a dear friend who races motorcycles on a full-time, professional level. He has ridden motorcycles at more than 200 miles per hour. Yet, at an early age, Reggie lost both of his legs below the knees and uses artificial limbs. In spite of the obvious challenges, Reggie is one of the most positive and inspiring people I have ever met. He never fails to encourage and motivate the people around him. Reggie frequently speaks to various youth groups and inner city kids, giving them a message of hope in their ability to overcome adversity. Yet the true power of Reggie's message is not in the content of his words but in the content of his character and in his incredible attitude of thankfulness that is reflected in his joyful spirit.

The secret is learning to be thankful *in* all things—not necessarily for all things. There are many things for which I am not thankful. But in spite of them, I still maintain an ongoing attitude of thankfulness. And so can you. Even when that discourteous driver cuts you off on the freeway. And, yes, even when you feel like advising him (in the spirit of Thanksgiving) to take his turkey and stuff it!

A great way to evaluate your "thankfulness quotient" is to honestly answer this question: Do you spend more time thinking about what you want in life than you do being thankful for what you have? We need to seek a "gratitude attitude." This means living a life of thankfulness, externalizing our gratefulness to others, and learning to be thankful in all things. It really does work!

Give the gift of a grateful heart today. Let the meaningful people in your life know how much you appreciate them. You'll be glad you did!

Sprint Cars

23

Two Common Lies

I like to believe that people are basically honest and trustworthy. But in spite of my belief in people's forthrightness, I have discovered that some people are often less than honest. In fact, I have discovered two lies that most people tell every day of their lives. Lie 1: "How are you?" Lie 2: "Fine, thank you."

Have you ever questioned the sincerity of concern when someone asks how you are? This courteous inquiry has become more of a cultural greeting than a sincere expression of concern for a person's well-being. If you give the inquirer a sob-story answer, many times you can watch the sincere concern melt into awkward discomfort. There is an unspoken law in our western culture that assumes no one will ever take this question seriously and attempt to answer it honestly. Most of us are also guilty of prolonging this charade of false concern by responding with our own "white" lie: "Fine, thank you."

When I became involved in racing, I discovered a totally new phenomena in this regard. Being a person of compassion and one who is legitimately concerned about people, I usually inquire as to the personal well-being of my racing friends when I see them. Here's my surprising discovery: Nine times out of ten, when I ask racers how they are, I receive an updated report on the status of their race team. In responding to my greeting, some racers can't even answer the question without first giving me a complete car performance report—something for which I didn't even ask. This leads me to a very interesting conclusion. Often a racer's emotional well-being is dictated by the most recent performance of his or her race car.

Once the racing season comes to an end, I can picture in my mind hundreds of racers walking around in sheer panic, not knowing how they are. I fully expect to call one of my friends during the winter and, after asking how he is doing, get the following response: "Ask me next year after the season begins. I should know by then."

Well, let's get one thing straight: *Performance does not determine worth.* When racers fall into a performance slump (which happens to everyone at some time), it's amazing to me how many of them begin to feel worthless. They question their ability, they second-guess their decisions, and occasionally they even question their value as a human being. (It's amazing how much instant healing comes from one good race.)

I remember well how, prior to 1987, people pondered how champion drag racer Dick LaHaie was able to race so successfully as a nonsponsored independent and actually make a living at it. I also recall Dick's personal philosophy, which he often shared: "Never let your wallet be controlled by your ego." Well said, Dick! In the same way, never let your happiness be controlled by your performance. Don't let your happiness or sense of worth be dictated by a time slip. It's a sad commentary when we allow a mere hundredth-of-a-second or one-mile-per-hour to determine our joy in life. So here's a good rule to live by: "Never let anything or anyone be in charge of your happiness." True happiness should always remain in your control as a reflection of your attitudes and values.

From my experience counseling with people for 30 years, I've discovered that only loving relationships, a proper self-image, and strong spiritual values provide true happiness. Racing can bring incredible satisfaction. It also promotes a sense of accomplishment and provides tremendous pleasure. But it cannot be the source of ultimate happiness. To seek that from racing or any other sport creates a false expectation that no endeavor can produce.

I believe it was billionaire J. Paul Getty who was once asked, "How much money is enough?" His reply was, "Just a little more." We should ask ourselves a similar question. How many wins are enough? How many wins are necessary for true happiness? Fifty? One hundred? Sadly, I can cite numerous examples of people who believe success leads to true happiness. Unfortunately, a deep, fulfilling joy never happens this way. Too often our need to succeed is driven by wrong motivations. And too often it results in further disappointment and only a momentary satisfaction. Our jobs can even become convenient places to hide from the need to find happiness elsewhere. I love racing. I think it is one of the greatest sports on earth. But it's not the purpose for living. Enjoy what you do but keep it in proper perspective.

If success doesn't provide lasting happiness, what does? I am reminded of Psalm 20:7 NIV, which says, "Some trust in chariots and some in horses, but we trust in the name of the LORD our God." The Israelites of the Old Testament often found themselves in battle, and it was during these times that they had to determine the focus of their trust. When they trusted in chariots and horses (man's provisions), they usually failed in battle. However, when they recognized *God* as the source and focus of their trust, they were victorious and ultimately satisfied. I am convinced that people who enjoy the greatest happiness are those who also have learned to find happiness outside of their careers. Racers, for instance, are dream chasers—driving toward the dream of winning the "big one." I admire the commitment demanded by such a valiant pursuit, but seeking wins as a hope of finding true happiness is not chasing a dream; it is chasing an illusion.

Genuine happiness comes as a result of relationships, a good self-image, and strong spiritual values. Joy is God's personal gift to you.

Mark Pawuk and His Pro Stock Pontiac

24

Coping with Tragedy

W*hy?* No other question reveals the anguish of tragedy like this single-syllable inquiry. Having been a minister for many years, I've been granted the opportunity of helping people face the tragedy of death on many occasions. While never a pleasant experience, I have repeatedly seen God comfort the human heart from the hurt that we encounter during such times.

How can hurting people be helped during a crisis that involves death? I use such opportunities to turn their hearts toward God and his perspective.

The Bible teaches that Christ was sent into this world that we might have life, and that we might have it more abundantly. God is a God of life; he is concerned about us and wants us to know and enjoy life as fully as possible. But the Bible also teaches that due to mankind's moral fall from the beginning of time, people throughout earth's history would be subject to death. It was therefore appointed that man would one day face death— not because God desired it, but because we are accountable as a race for the consequences of our free will as demonstrated by Adam and Eve in the garden of Eden.

Death entered our world because of man's wrong—not because of God's choice. In fact, to prove how much he desired life above death for his creation, Jesus Christ was sent to die in our place in order that we might experience new life, here and hereafter, through his sacrifice on the cross (Sunday School 101).

God allows us the freedom of doing what we please in life, whether he approves of it or not. If we do things that contain a high risk factor, then we are responsible for the consequences of that added level of risk. Many people have paid such a price in years past—be it from motor racing, skydiving, football, or even from driving to the supermarket. Not one of us has a guarantee beyond our next breath of air. Death is a part of life we must accept whether we understand it or not, whether we like it or not. We can only minimize the possibility by keeping ourselves out of high risk situations.

To those courageous racers who have lost their lives in years past, avoiding that risk was never an acceptable option. They knew the potential risks and willingly faced them. As mortal beings, we cannot ignore the principle of cause and effect, which simply means some things will go wrong on occasion. Accidents do happen, and we are all vulnerable to this ongoing axiom of life. We must therefore accept the consequences and enjoy life as fully as we can.

I believe with all my heart that in every tragedy there is an answer to the question why. I also believe, however, that in very few instances will we ever know or be able to comprehend that answer. Thus, my advice to those who want to know why is to not ask that question.

God never promised we would know the secrets of the ages or understand the reasoning behind every event in history. He did, however, say, "Will not the Judge of all the earth do right?" (Genesis 18:25 NIV). In that implied promise we must learn to trust, and trust means we do not always know the end result or see the ultimate purpose in life's many scenarios.

Having been around racing for 40 years, I have often heard a common statement among lovers of speed and competition.

Almost without exception racers say, "If I have to die some day, let me be doing what I love in life." For those who have lost their lives in motor racing, that wish became a reality just as they desired.

The bottom line is that none of us gets to determine whether or not he or she will experience physical death. The only choices available to us is whether we will be prepared to face death when it comes, choose to ignore death, or try to convince ourselves of personal invincibility—and that's a losing game every time. That's where perspective comes in. Biblical truth says we need to be prepared. For instance, Romans 8:6 (NIV) states, "The mind of sinful man is death, but the mind controlled by the Spirit is life and peace." And remember what the man said in the parable of the landowner with abundant crops, "…I'll say to myself, 'You have plenty of good things laid up for many years. Take life easy; eat, drink and be merry.' But God said to him, 'You fool! This very night your life will be demanded from you. Then who will get what you have prepared for yourself?'" (Luke 12:19-20 NIV).

What should we do in our lives today to be ready for death? "You ought to live holy and godly lives" (2 Peter 3:11 NIV) and "make every effort to be found spotless, blameless and at peace with [God]" (2 Peter 3:14 NIV). This way we can present ourselves to God as approved, workers who do not need to be ashamed and who correctly handle the word of truth (see 2 Timothy 2:15 NIV). Be knowledgeable about God's truth and understand his wisdom.

A story is told of two people—an uncivilized tribal bushman and a medical student—watching a surgeon perform the amputation of a man's leg due to severe gangrene.

To the bushman who does not understand medical procedures or amputations, what he witnesses in the removal of the man's leg is to him an act of cruelty and violence. He does not understand how anything so tragic could be done to this seemingly innocent person lying helplessly on the operating table. The medical student next to him, however, sees the same situation from an entirely different perspective. Because he understands the results of gangrene and realizes that the patient's life is in danger if the leg is not removed, he sees the surgeon's behavior as an act of kindness and mercy.

Two people witness the exact same event and have opposite reactions. What determines the difference? The difference is in their perspectives. The med student had knowledge that helped him realize that the amputation was going to save the patient's life, therefore it was an act of mercy, not of violence. The bushman, without benefit of that knowledge, could only see the event as cruel and violent.

In many of life's tragic scenarios and events we make our conclusions and responses based on limited knowledge. God the Almighty, with his unlimited knowledge, sees things from a different perspective than we do. This brings us back to trust. "Will not the Judge of all the earth do right?" In times of tragedy and personal loss, we need only call on God's strength and comfort and learn to trust him.

Loss of life is never easy or pleasant to cope with, but we who remain must gain beneficial results from such tragedies, lest those who die, do so in vain. Perhaps you have lost people in your life recently. People who wanted to contribute to making this world a better place. It's up to you to determine if their ability to influence this world for good will continue. Their lives can still produce positive results in our lives today—if we allow them to. May the people who have died rest in peacefulness with our heavenly Father as we faithfully carry on with their loving memories in our hearts.

25

Rules Are Not for Cheaters

With all due respect to David Letterman, the most famous "Top-10 List" in history was written by God several thousand years ago. Certainly the most famous, but not necessarily the most popular. Intrinsic in our human nature seems to be a stubbornness to resist rules. We do not like being told what—and what not—to do.

Man brings very little into this world from birth, but one thing he brings is a self-centered orientation that ultimately expresses itself as selfishness. At some point in the growth process, that strong willful spirit must be broken into submission before obedience and civility can become a practical reality in a person's life.

Unfortunately, that stubborn willfulness never goes away completely. It forever challenges our capricious efforts to bring it under control. I suppose that's why we abhor rules so much; everyone knows rules take away the fun in life. So why are they necessary, anyway?

God's Top-10—direct from his office atop Mount Sinai—are known as the Ten Commandments. They were meant to serve as guidelines for man's ultimate good and happiness. Or, as some might say, the top-10 ways to guarantee true happiness and fulfillment in life. We must remember that they're the Ten Commandments *not* the Ten Suggestions.

Without a doubt, the regulations that come from racing's tech and rules committees are designed for a driver's safety and to ensure that he or she will be able to receive the greatest amount of enjoyment from the sport. From the way some racers talk, however, you would think that rules limit all the fun at the track. But rules are operational guidelines to guarantee that everyone has an equal opportunity to perform within the limits of safety and are assured of the maximum enjoyment that comes from competing against others on a fair and equal basis.

Unfortunately, there will always be some people who feel they need an advantage over others. These folks are usually willing to break the rules in order to attain that advantage. This is selfishness by people who have never considered it important to bring their willfulness under control and submission. And, whether in racing or in daily living, they are the ones who cause problems for the rest of us.

If laws are broken, rules serve another purpose. They become the standard of comparison by which the lawbreaker is judged and found guilty of disobedience. The same law, which was never created with cheaters in mind, becomes the means of evaluation and judgment. Whether we're talking about God or any racing organization (and, yes, there is a difference), the result is often suspension. Fortunately, both systems have a process of appeal and a procedure for reinstatement once certain conditions are met. There are consequences to breaking laws. Without consequences, laws merely become advice. That's why a racer's rulebook is not a book of advice. It's a book of rules! Rules with power behind them. It's also the reason God's Rulebook is more than just a book of advice.

A racer's rulebook was primarily written to create a safe and enjoyable sport in which we can all participate. God's rules were written with the same intent. Follow his guidelines and you will be assured of the maximum safety and enjoyment life can offer. Disobey his rules and there are significant consequences.

No one enjoys imposing judgment on lawbreakers. Not God; not any racing body. Any director of racing and competition will tell you that judgment is essential to protect and maintain the integrity of the sport. God agrees. As long as some choose to disobey, judgment and restriction will be necessary. Eliminate (or even minimize) those consequences, and the whole system soon crumbles.

There is a very important verse of scripture in the Old Testament. It's found in Deuteronomy 6:24 NASB and says, "the LORD commanded us to observe all these statutes, to fear the LORD our God for our good always." Conversely, when we disobey, the results are not in our best interests, and consequences will be necessary as a means of protecting the integrity of the system. And always remember: The greatest consequence is not in the judgment imposed, but rather the lack of "good" that obedience would have brought in the first place. Think about it.

Without question, the most satisfied person in racing is the one who succeeds and obeys the rules. Likewise, the happiest person in life is the one who finds that success and fulfillment come as a result of following God's guidelines. Ah, the joys of obedience!

SCCA Road Racing

26

Joy to the World

For so many people their favorite time of the year is the month of December because it means Christmas is just around the corner. Everyone loves Christmas because it's a traditional time of joyfulness and happiness—from decorations and Christmas cards to the carols we sing in preparation for that wonderful day.

Although I'm not going to discuss the Christmas season, I do want to comment on "joy to the world." This is not just a Christmas message; it's also a lifelong goal.

Most people are understandably concerned with happiness in their lives, but you may be surprised to learn that the Bible has very little to say about our happiness. In fact, I have learned that God isn't all that concerned whether we experience happiness or not. He does, however, want us to know the *power of joyfulness*. The difference is significant.

In studying the biblical difference between joy and happiness, I was quite surprised by the way the Bible treats these two subjects. If you look at the dictionary meaning of happy, you will discover that it means: "to be favored by circumstances, to be lucky or fortunate." It comes from the root word "hap," which means "by luck or chance."

Happiness is usually considered and experienced by most people as an emotion, and since it comes from the word "happenings," it is therefore an emotion dependent upon certain things or events taking place in your life. Just think how often you hear people say, "I'll be happy as long as _____" or "I could be happy if only _____."

Here's some of the best advice I can ever give: Never let anything or anyone be in charge of your happiness. Your happiness should always be founded in your personal values and your personal relationships with God and others. Once you abdicate the responsibility for your happiness to anyone or anything else, you can be assured that you will never experience real joy on any consistent or meaningful level.

The Bible presents joy as a choice—a chosen *state* of attitude. True joy is not dependent upon certain feelings, material possessions, or events in your life. It is the result of specific choices. And to my utter dismay, there are people who, for whatever reasons, still refuse to follow that chosen path of joyfulness. But it doesn't have to be that way. I have discovered in my years of experiencing life that we can have true joy and not even be happy. Yes, true joy has nothing to do with happiness. That's why our joy should never be affected by circumstances. In fact, there are times when our greatest joys can even come out of times of suffering.

My friend Darrell Gwynn was tragically paralyzed in a racing accident a number of years ago. He has been an incredible inspiration to me and others in regard to joy. Darrell isn't happy with the circumstances and happenings of his life that paralyzed him, but with God's grace he has chosen to live a life filled with joy in spite of those circumstances. He decided to make that choice, and as I see the results of it working in his life, it raises me to new levels of inspiration.

Joy isn't affected by circumstances. And even though there are pleasant emotions that accompany joy, remember that joy is not dependent upon emotions. That's why when emotions change or depart (which they're prone to do), joy still remains.

I love the philosophy espoused by former drag racer Eddie Hill (a philosophy put to severe tests many times in his racing career). I often heard Eddie say that he refused to let his emotions be dictated by the performance of his race car. That's a lesson that every racer needs to learn—and learn well. What my precious friend discovered is that achieving "Low Elapsed Time" brings a few moments of happiness, but not lasting joyfulness. It's not morally wrong to seek happiness, of course, but never let it become a replacement for true joy.

One well-known professional racer who has one of the best records for winning in all of motorsports sat down with a friend of mine in the midst of his extensive collection of championship trophies. He looked around and asked, "Is this all there is to life?" This man had everything the world claims is necessary for ultimate happiness: fame, fortune, and all the glorious trappings. But he still lacked true joy—and the absence of that joy left within him a deep feeling of emptiness.

The Bible word for joy is the root word for grace, which means "gift." Like grace, joy is a gift from God. It must be received as a gift and activated in our lives. That's why Christian people have an inside track on knowing true joy. But any gift is useless unless it is received and activated. Remember also that joy is a gift that can be given. Have you given the gift of joy to anyone recently?

Since the Bible is the best source for understanding joy, I want to also point out that it describes joy as a fruit of the Spirit (Galatians 5:22). What does this tell us about joy? Good fruit comes as a result of proper care and occasional pruning, so joy isn't always the result of happy circumstances. Furthermore, the purpose of fruit is to feed and nourish. Does the joyfulness of your life nurture others?

When I examine the world around me, I see far too many people looking to possessions and to other people for the elusive feeling of happiness—and continually coming up empty. What I pray they will one day discover is that joy in the Bible is not an emotion or a feeling but a growing characteristic of the Christian life. That's why you can take away my possessions and you can even take away my happiness—but you can't take away my joy!

So let joy be an active force in your life; let it be in control. Emotions are basically responsive and reactionary expressions, but choices were designed to guide your life. Likewise, happiness is merely a reaction to what happens around you, while joy is a dynamic, controlling force. As you look to each new day, commit to live a life filled with joy to the world.

part four

INSPIRATION

Tony Pedregon's Funny Car at 310 MPH

27

The Ant, the Prayer, and the Contact Lens

The following is a true story (as told by Josh Zarandona) about a young woman named Brenda who was invited to go rock climbing with her friends. Although she was scared to death, she went with her group to a large granite cliff. In spite of her fear, she put on her climbing gear, took hold of the rope, and started up the face of the rock.

When she got to a ledge, she decided to take a breather. As she was hanging there for a few moments, the safety rope snapped, hitting Brenda's eye and knocking out her contact lens. Suddenly she was on a rock ledge with hundreds of feet below her and hundreds of feet above her. She looked and looked, hoping the contact lens had landed on the ledge in front of her, but it was nowhere to be found.

Reality soon set in. Here she was, far from home, hanging on a cliff, and seeing everything as a blur. She was desperate and began to get upset, so she prayed to God to help her find the lens. When she managed to get to the next level, a friend examined her eye and clothing, but there was no contact lens.

Despondent, she sat down with members of the party, waiting for the rest of the team to make it up the face of the cliff. She looked out across range after range of mountains, thinking of the Bible verse that says: "The eyes of the LORD run to and fro throughout the whole earth" (2 Chronicles 16:9 KJV). She thought, *Lord, you can see all these mountains. You know every stone and leaf, and you know exactly where my contact lens is. Please help me.*

Finally, they walked back down via a trail. At the bottom there was a new party of climbers just starting up the face of the cliff. One of them shouted, "Hey, you guys! Anybody lose a contact lens?" That would be startling enough, but they were really amazed upon hearing how the climber found it. An ant was moving slowly across the face of the rock carrying the lens.

Brenda later told the story to her father, a cartoonist. When he heard the incredible story of the ant, the prayer, and the contact lens, he drew a picture of an ant lugging a contact lens with the following caption, "Lord, I don't know why you want me to carry this thing. I can't eat it, and it's awfully heavy. But if this is what you want me to do, I'll carry it for you."

It would probably do most of us good to occasionally voice a similar prayer: "God, I don't know why you want me to carry this load. I can see no good in it, and it's quite wearying. But if you want me to carry it, I will."

I am a firm believer that there are times in our lives when God calls us to do things we do not comprehend, things that cause us to endure some of the weighty matters of life.

The ant in the story never understood the significance of its actions. And whether its motives were benevolent or not isn't the issue. God used the ant's willingness and energy to answer a very specific prayer from a blurry-eyed, rookie rock climber named Brenda.

There are so many people around us who are going through life in a fog, crying for help and trying to make sense of unfortunate circumstances. I wonder how often God challenges us to endure some unpleasant burden that he wishes to utilize as the answer to someone's prayer or to meet someone's need. Though many people go through life oblivious to the privilege of such opportunities, whenever challenging experiences are accompanied by a willing heart and a positive attitude, God graciously allows us some insight at an appropriate time as to the beneficial results of these experiences.

I am a firm believer that these opportunities are an occasional part of every individual's life. It is my fervent prayer that the day will come when we will be able to see and understand some of the positive effects of the greatness that God wants to model to the world through us. If we can maintain our focus along with a willing and positive attitude, we will be a blessing and inspiration to others beyond any level of our imagination.

Without question it was God who caused a rock climber to notice an ant carrying a contact lens. And without question it is the same God who will one day cause a blurry-eyed world to take notice of the extraordinary greatness and courage that he has instilled in many Christians. God doesn't call the qualified. He qualifies the called. Are you hearing the call?

28

Old Mules, Mud Puddles, and Dandelions

A farmer owned an old mule. One day the mule fell into the farmer's well. After carefully assessing the situation, the farmer sympathized with the mule but decided that neither the mule nor the well was worth the trouble of saving. He called his neighbors together and told them what had happened and then he enlisted them to help haul dirt to bury the old mule in the well and put him out of his misery.

Initially, the old mule was hysterical. But as the farmer and friends continued shoveling dirt onto the mule's back, a thought struck the mule. It suddenly occurred to him that every time a shovel load of dirt landed on his back he should shake it off and step up.

So this is what he did, blow after blow. With every shovel load of dirt, the old mule chose to shake it off and step up, shake it off and step up, shake it off and step up.

No matter how painful the blows or how distressing the situation seemed to be, the old mule fought the sense of panic and continued to shake off the dirt and step up.

Amazingly, it wasn't long before the old mule, battered and exhausted, stepped triumphantly over the wall of the well and onto solid ground.

The very crisis that seemed likely to bury the mule actually blessed him and became his deliverance all because of the manner in which he handled his adversity.

The same is true in our lives as well. If we face our problems and respond to them positively—refusing to submit to panic, bitterness, or self-pity—we will discover that the adversities that come to bury us usually have within them the potential to benefit and bless us. Oftentimes it's merely a matter of attitude and perspective.

With every circumstance comes the privilege of choice. We can choose to see the negative sides of situations or we can choose to see the positive sides. This is a wonderful gift God has bestowed upon us as part of our free will. Unfortunately, seeing the negative side seems to be mankind's basic default-system. In other words, unless we deliberately choose to see the positive and the good in unfortunate circumstances, we tend to automatically respond to the negative side in most situations. The good news, however, is that we have full control over our reactions! We can choose to change our default system. We can't avoid adversity in life. From foul starts to blown engines, from broken parts to malfunctioning electronics, we are forced to face the challenges of racing and life. Let's determine to face those challenges with a positive and mature attitude.

The following story has always inspired and challenged me. I hope it will do the same for you. The author—no doubt an experienced parent—is unknown. But for me, this story tends to put things in proper perspective and serves as an important reminder to choose to see things in a new way.

> When I look at a patch of dandelions, I see a bunch of weeds that are trying to take over my yard. My kids, however, see flowers for mom and white fluff you can blow and wish on.

When I look at an old drunk smiling at me, I see a smelly, dirty person who probably wants money, and I look away. My kids see a potential friend, and they smile back.

When I hear music that I love, I know I can't carry a tune and don't have much rhythm, so I sit self-consciously and listen. My kids feel the beat and dance to it. They sing out the words. And if they don't know the words, they create their own.

When I feel wind on my face, I brace myself against it. I feel it messing up my hair and pushing me back when I walk. My kids close their eyes, spread their arms and try to fly, until they fall to the ground laughing.

When I pray, I say thee and thou and grant me this and give me that. My kids say, "Hi, God! Thanks for my toys and my friends. Please keep the bad dreams away tonight."

When I see a mud puddle, I step around it. I see muddy shoes and dirty carpets. My kids sit in it. They see dams to build, rivers to cross, and boats to float.

I wonder if parents are given kids to teach or to learn from? No wonder God "loves the little children of the world."

So, enjoy the little things in life—for one day you may look back and realize that they became the big things.

29

Swollen Bodies and
Shriveled Wings

We can never avoid all adversity. Like it or not, it is part of life on earth. But there is good news: Adversity is what God often uses to help us grow. Adversity will toughen us in a constructive way and challenge every area of weak character in our lives.

God does not author our problems or cause our adversities, but I believe he is always willing to use those unfortunate circumstances in our lives to develop maturity and character within us. No doubt, every one of you can relate to some adverse situation in your life from which you learned important lessons, in spite of the pain and discomfort. Life can be a very effective instructor if we learn to approach it with an open mind and a desire to grow.

To this day, I can still remember once discovering the cocoon of a butterfly. One day a small opening appeared, and—as a curious and concerned young boy—I watched the butterfly for several hours as it struggled to force its body through a little hole in the cocoon.

Then it seemed to stop making any progress. It appeared as if it had gotten as far as it could and could go no farther.

In my compassion I decided to help the butterfly. I took a pair of scissors and snipped off the remaining bit of the cocoon. The butterfly emerged quite easily. But to my surprise, it had a swollen body and small, underdeveloped wings.

I continued to watch the butterfly because I expected that, at any moment, the wings would become enlarged and expand enough to support the body, which (I assumed) would begin to shrink in time.

Neither happened. In fact, the butterfly spent the rest of the afternoon and probably its life crawling around with a swollen body and shriveled wings. It couldn't fly.

What I didn't understand in my innocence and haste was that the restricting cocoon and the struggle required for the butterfly to get through that tiny opening were God's way of forcing fluid from the body of the butterfly into its wings so that it would be ready for flight once it escaped from the cocoon.

Sometimes struggles are exactly what we need. If God allowed us to go through life without any obstacles or adversities, it would cripple us. We would not be as strong as we could have been as a result of our adversities. There are no doubt hundreds of racers within our sport who can testify to the fact that adversity has made them better racers—and even better people. I'm sure that given the choice, most of us would opt to avoid adversities altogether. We would remain content to crawl through life with swollen bodies and shriveled wings—even when God wants to prepare us to fly above our misfortunes.

Have you ever wondered why so many people root for the underdog in racing? It's because we admire those people who have successfully overcome adversity. Perhaps in some small way we vicariously identify with those people, gaining some measure of encouragement that we, too, can overcome the challenging circumstances of our lives.

At some point in life, we all become the "little guy." We become David battling every Goliath life throws before us. And it is our constant hope that we, too, can beat the odds. Like a beautiful butterfly overcoming its struggle to free itself from its cocoon, God wants us to learn to fly in total freedom. But like the butterfly, we will never be able to soar above our circumstances without first enduring those challenges in life that are necessary to strengthen our wings.

Kebin Kinsley Driving a 200+ MPH Top Fuel Hydro Drag Boat

30

Changing Priorities

I remember reading a very profound statement, the truth of which has never escaped me. The statement was quite simple in its essence, yet extremely penetrating in its depth of understanding. It profoundly proclaimed the following perspective on life: "Children rejoice in what they *have*—youth rejoice in what they *do*—and adults rejoice in what they *are*." Within this one unpretentious statement we clearly see in simplistic wisdom the changing priorities of life...from possessions to accomplishments to character.

Even from our youngest years of childhood, we quickly attached ourselves to things—a pacifier, a teething ring, a blanket. As children we derived our joy from things we could touch and hold. As a youngster, I focused on building model cars. It brought rejoicing into my life and some frustration when the parts wouldn't cooperate.

As I grew into my teen years, I began to rejoice in accomplishments. Being an "A" student, earning my letter on the baseball team, or graduating as valedictorian of my class brought great joy. (I'll let you guess which two are true.)

Obviously, many of us are living proof that this adolescent need for accomplishment often carries well into adulthood. Like having the fastest car, owning the nicest boat, or buying the biggest house. (Did I mention having the fastest car?)

But one of the wonderful advantages to becoming a Christian is the amazing way that God helps us in our character development. Some refer to this process as personal discipleship, and in the course of growing and maturing in Christ, I believe the development of maturity and character growth is increased significantly.

At some point as we approach adulthood a fascinating change takes place within us. Not only do possessions slowly lose their previous importance, but even our accomplishments in life do not seem quite as significant as they once did. It's at this unpredictable point in life that we find ourselves becoming strangely satisfied with "who" we are—something we never thought would be so important to us.

But how can this be? Aren't we taught that the person with the most toys wins? So why am I now asking myself, "Wins what?" I guess we never considered that question to be relevant before. After all, it didn't really matter what we won, as long as we won. That was the goal. And winning, we were told, was accomplished by gathering the most things.

Before long, we begin to engage in a systematic inventory of the accomplishments of our lives. During our earlier years of youthfulness, we were filled with dreams. We were challenged by great visions. We still had the potential to be great, to be somebody special, to do something of true significance.

But then we awaken one morning to the realization that we haven't changed the world, we didn't discover a cure for cancer, and we probably won't be nominated for a Nobel prize. And perhaps being a wealthy, successful racer is even out of the question.

But we also realize that it's okay. Maybe our life wasn't as exciting as we once envisioned, but neither was it all that bad.

That's when "it" happens. *Who would have thought? Who knew this could ever transpire? We suddenly realize that we actually like being who we are.* There's a strange sense of satisfaction as we objectively consider the journey that has brought us to this point. And with this satisfaction comes the reality that this newly found realization is not at all based on the number of things we have accumulated in life nor is it a result of a long list of personal accomplishments that may adorn our resumé.

No, it's more than that. Perhaps it's hard to define or articulate, but we know it's there, somewhere deep within us. It's very real. In fact, it's far more real than any of the things or accomplishments we once thought were so essential to a successful and meaningful life. And though we might not think to describe this new revelation with this particular word, we nevertheless begin to find subtle expressions of rejoicing over this profound awareness.

If I were to summarize in one word this process of life that takes us from childhood to adulthood, I would choose the word "character." And it is in our perception of this process that character is ultimately defined within our world of moral awareness. Character is a result of values. And our values will be a result of the way we respond to the various stages of the process from childhood to adulthood. In the end, character is all that matters. In the end, character is all that will remain.

We progress on this journey at differing paces. The transition from one stage to the next is not a function of age but a *function of maturity*. It is not so much a result of the events of our lives; it's more a result of the choices of our lives. Some may reach "adulthood" in their 20s or 30s. Others may one day sit on their front porch in tranquil retirement, quite unaware that such a journey even existed.

Have you ever known a racer or someone else who measures his or her sense of importance by the number of trophies on the mantel? Too often such a person is never satisfied with gaining more trophies. And this person never seems to reach a place of contentment, let alone joyfulness, as a result of further accomplishments. An emptiness exists because winning is never enough. Rather than developing meaningful character, this person is driven to seek another trophy, another championship.

I certainly admire and commend the dedication and drive necessary to be a consistent winner, but if winning doesn't bring the sense of personal satisfaction you seek in life, perhaps it's time to consider the transition to a higher priority. Measure your self-worth by who you are, not by what you accomplish. This doesn't mean you can't enjoy winning. Continue to strive for perfection, but seek fulfillment in the process of developing character.

Here's the bottom line. We all journey through this process. The things of childhood pass away, and then the accomplishments fade. What you once did that was meaningful to you will one day come to a meaningless end. Only what you are will remain. Is what you are today enough to satisfy you through the years of life ahead? I trust the answer is yes.

Enjoy the journey!

31

Value Determines Choice

I have always been a strong believer in this axiom. Value determines choice. I see this as a concept basic to all humanity and placed within us from birth. When we perceive something to be of worth, its intrinsic value demands that we choose it. This is one of the primary reasons that I choose to obey God and serve him fully. I see his value as being clearly greater than anything else in life. I don't want to settle for less.

Based on our perception of value, the most valuable object or principle says, "Choose me." For example, let's assume you are a racer who entered and won a raffle for a free engine for your race car. According to the rules of the raffle, you are able to select one of two engines. The first engine is a stock Chevy V8. A good solid motor that is rated at 250 horsepower. The second engine available to you is a full-race, high-performance race motor that registered more than 500 horsepower on a dynamometer. As an astute race car driver and mechanic, which of these two motors would you select?

You would likely select the second motor because you would view it as being more valuable to your racing program and your desire for more power. However, what we understand of value is often limited. Let us suppose, for example, that I forgot to tell you that the second motor had a flawed block and was built with inferior quality engine parts that might fail under severe stress. Want to change your selection?

You see, values change with the acquisition of additional knowledge. This is precisely how God challenges our values—by reasoning with us that there is a higher level of understanding and values to live by. When necessary, God uses knowledge to shape our values. He uses influence rather than force. This is why the ultimate essence of the Christian faith is a belief that God is the most valuable thing in existence. Therefore, wisdom *obligates* us to seek to serve him fully. Serving God makes the most sense.

To an adherent of the Christian faith, values and absolutes are founded in God's character and are intrinsic to his nature. They are not established arbitrarily. God values patience because he is patient. He values justice because he is just. He values love because he is loving. Furthermore, perceived value leads to incentive and motivation. Your own spiritual growth will develop no higher than your understanding of the value of God and his precepts. In other words, you will never be motivated beyond the limits of what you perceive to be of value in life.

What About You?

I want to ask you two very important questions. What do you perceive as the most valuable thing in existence? Have you ever developed a personal relationship with God?

It has been my privilege to help hundreds of racers and crews discover the fact that God is the most valuable being in the universe. Based on that realization, they have discovered that serving him is the most intelligent decision a human being can make. It's logical. It makes the most sense. It's not about feeling good, although there is no greater feeling than knowing you are one with God. It's about doing the right thing. Doing the sensible thing. Doing the best thing. And making the most reasonable choice you can make! It is God's desire to reveal himself to you so that you, too, will see this as the wisest and best thing that could ever happen in your life. If you do not currently know God on that level, I pray that you will open your heart and allow him to make himself known to you in that way. He will be faithful to do so.

Racing is all about winning and achieving victory. So is life. And when we commit our lives to God, we discover the greatest victory known to man. It is the ultimate winning experience, and God will personally escort you to the winner's circle of life as you celebrate together. Then he will present to you the greatest prize possible—the gift of eternal life.

While the start of any race is important, the most critical aspect of winning is how a driver finishes the race. Life is much the same. How you cross the finish line is the most important concern. Perhaps the start of your life was not what you would have preferred. Perhaps your spiritual progress toward ultimate victory has been marred and hindered by a few crashes and some sloppy pit stops along the way. The good news is that you have not yet reached the finish line. It's not too late to turn your life over to Christ, put him in the driver's seat, and ride with him to the finish line where you can join him in the victory circle for eternity. It's the only victory that truly matters.

Are you...
Crazy
About Cars?

Do you chronicle your personal history according to which make and model you were driving at the time? Do you take the long way through a parking lot just to maneuver the speed bumps twice? If you are certifiably crazy about cars, then cruise along with this fuel-injected look at life—it comes standard with freedom, power, and faith in what lies beyond the open road.

A backdrop of colorful, gleaming, classic automobiles will remind you of the greatest destination of all—the driver's seat of your favorite car.

Cars create a special kind of emotion in the lives of those who own them and care for them. It may be quite difficult to explain at times, but then again, who has ever been able to explain love?

—Ken Owens, president
Racers For Christ

Other Good
Harvest House Reading

A Look at Life from a Deer Stand
Steve Chapman

Taking you on his successful and not-so-successful hunts, Chapman shares the skills for successful hunting—and living. With excitement and humor, he shares the parallels between hunting and walking with God.

With God on a Deer Hunt
Steve Chapman

Capturing the excitement of matching wits with elusive whitetail, Steve invites you into the joy of God's presence. Through often-humorous adventures, readers will discover keen insights and biblical truths that come with spending time outdoors.

With God on the Hiking Trail
Nathan Chapman

Narrow paths, mountain-top experiences, hunger, fulfillment…Nathan explores the parallels between walking with God and walking in the outdoors in this collection of devotional meditations. Perfectly sized for packing along on a trek or trail.

With God on the Open Road
Steve Chapman

Ever notice how loud, steady background noise contributes to calm thought and reflection? Steve Chapman has. It's the basis of this devotional for motorcycle enthusiasts. Discover the hymns found in the hum of the road!

I Used to Have Answers, Now I Have Kids
Phil Callaway

These sparkling, warmly told stories capture the amusing and bemusing experiences of life while sharing timeless spiritual lessons. Funny and inspiring, Phil reminds us that it's wonderful to be part of a family.

Men Are Like Waffles—Women Are Like Spaghetti
Bill and Pam Farrel

Men keep life elements in separate boxes; women intertwine everything. Providing biblical insights, sound research, and humorous anecdotes, the Farrels explore gender differences and preferences and how they can strengthen relationships. Be sure to also get the companion book, *Men Are Like Waffles, Women Are Like Spaghetti Study Guide.*

The Things That Matter Most
Bob Welch

These sparkling stories about the things that matter most—family, love, character, and faith—reveal our deep longing for trust and meaning, and remind us that God is the true source of contentment.